So That's How They Do It!

TACTICS OF BUSINESS MASTERS

I0470114

By Bart Jackson

Published by

BartsBooks

A division of Prometheus Publishing, LLC

Published in the United States by
Prometheus Publishing, LLC
Please address all queries to Prometheus Publishing,
P.O. Box 534, Cranbury, New Jersey 08512

Prometheus Publishing books are available at special rates
for bulk purchases. Contact the publisher at the above address.

ISBN – 13:978-148182-4521
ISBN – 10:148182452X

© January, 2013

BartsBooks Ultimate Business Guides
Prometheus Publishing, LLC

Welcome to BartsBooks

Business unleashes each of our innate cravings to create. Further, it interweaves many individuals' talents, delivering useful entities for all. These are the exciting challenges of business. 'Tis heady stuff, and everyone has something of value to contribute. BartsBooks works to ignite this excitement in the business community. And by helping those involved better meet their challenges, BartsBooks strives to nudge business in fact and perception toward what it should be – a force for good.

BartsBooks' Ultimate Business Guides offer concise counsel from a broad collaboration of business masters. All are set in a succinct format that suits the tight schedules of those in the business community. We build each book on specialized topics with the help of select authorities and people who have experienced it all themselves – like you. We invite you to help us build the BartsBooks of your choice, by visiting www.BartsBooks.com.

1. Sculpting Yourself

2. Becoming Aware

3. Playing Profitably with Others

4. Enlisting Aid

5. Selling Your Abilities

6. Final Caveats

Roster of Authorities

Acknowledgments

Our grateful praise to the hundreds in the business community who contributed their many excellent ideas and made this volume possible.

Also sincerest thanks to Jeanne Murphy and her team of advisors, to Sharon Sheiman who thoughtfully reviewed each segment to help determine and present those of greatest value, and to editor Christian Kirkpatrick.

Blessings to Dorothy Amsden for her amazing graphic artistry, and to Carol Ezzo for her editorial comments and for attending to so many vital details.

Finally, heartfelt thanks to my wife Lorraine, who not only edits her husband's works, she edits him.

Introduction

Who's got the secret? What makes one person absolutely flourish in their business career, while the rest barely muddle along?

After we've cleared away all the excuses and circumstance – the right place, right time, part of the right network, naturally gifted patter, handsome, picked the right product, right team.... After all the secondary advantages have been seen for what they truly are: secondary – it all comes back to You.

Success and satisfaction – the stem and flower of each person's hopes – lie rooted within those mindsets, knowledge, disciplines, daring, and deeds that each of us can cultivate. You never hear lumberjacks complain that "some cutters have sharp axes and some don't." So instead of waiting for some divinely gifted head for business, we invite you to take out your whetstone. The sharper you hone your personal skills, the better you will be able to scythe down the obstacles and reap business's many rewards.

This volume is designed to help you do just that. It will guide you to putting a keen edge on body, mind, spirit, and even soul, so you might gain more from that major part of your life to which you devote so much. These pages are filled with tactics wrung from the hard-won experience of many business leaders. They have worked for these people. They might work for you. Or perhaps they will provide some clay from which you may sculpt your own improvement.

Some of these tactics are simple disciplines or clever techniques. Some involve profound insight. All demand changing your current routine and making an accompanying Attitude Adjustment. It is tragically futile to practice the trick of someone else's trade without your mind's understanding and your spirit's wholeheartedly backing it.

Because each new path holds its pitfalls, we embellish our tactics with Blunders to Avoid, plus a few Tips & Tasks to ease application. Each tactic will hopefully provide you a useful tool you can put to work in that volatile realm of your daily business – and perhaps something to help your life after hours. (May we never dice up our lives into separate boxes.)

Business entails an infinitely creative, but darn tough journey, and you will find no cheerleading promises in these pages. Many business people who prepare perfectly and strive gallantly will still fail. Such is life. Nor is this a business guide for dummies. If you are a dummy, best read elsewhere – and best avoid business. We are only helping you better the odds towards your vision of success.

As you read the techniques and ideas that have helped bring others forward, I would ask that you employ them not only as tools, but also as steps toward a loftier personal vision. Keep in mind the wisdom of Henry David Thoreau, heir to a Massachusetts pencil manufacturing fortune, who noted "In the end, most men (and women) hit what they aim at."

As with all BartsBooks, the insights in these pages come from a broad reaching collaboration. We have gathered wisdom from scores of business veterans and distilled their ideas into those tools we deem most vital. Our goal remains to present you succinctly the widest array of solutions from the greatest number of sources. From many minds flow more knowledge, and perhaps more importantly, newer perspectives. We invite you to visit www.BartsBooks.com and help build our books.

Wishing you every success, – Bart Jackson

Final thought...
You and I hold the collected wisdom of all those people
we have paused to appreciate.

×

CHAPTER 1

Sculpting Yourself

No true work of art is ever finished – it is merely abandoned.

Prelude

How marvelously resilient and adaptable we humans are.
We can modify thousands of tasks to suit ourselves. Equally, we can
accommodate ourselves in endless ways to better address our tasks.
And the cleverest among us can deduce which requires the adjustment.

This chapter rolls out several ways in which you can mold your
intricate assemblage of personal potential to better achieve your goals.
The examples range from unkinking a certain mindset and letting the
passion flow, to improving time or body management. The list is not,
nor ever can be complete. But hopefully, these few examples will spark
other adaptations that will better arm you for the complex onslaught
of business.

As you read, and consider your self-sculpting journey, please keep
the antennae ever searching. Every time you face an entangling, uphill
frustration, pause and ask, "Is this grind really necessary?" Some
tasks are unavoidably onerous, but often a little self-reinvention saves
oceans of sweat. There's almost always a better way, and almost
always it involves bringing your untapped resources to bear.

Step Back and Select

Holly Bull – CEO, The Center for Interim Programs

Nothing great has ever been achieved without enthusiasm. Repeated in myriad forms, this old maxim of Thoreau still holds true. The good news is that the avenues for this enthusiastic achievement have burgeoned exponentially. Our options today are boggling. Just 80 years ago, more than a quarter of all Americans labored on the family farm. Today, only a handful of occupations can claim to involve even five percent of the nation's total workforce. And even within each of those occupations, the variety of work varies drastically.

✳ **A Wider Lens.** Most all of us really want to follow our passion and work at what we love. Yes, we know that the array of choices stands wider than ever, but we still career hunt using the same narrow lens of our parents. There lies a far vaster globe open to you, my friend, than is e'er envisioned through the executive recruiter's scope.

Granted, exploring the full limits for your exact-fit job now takes more time, effort, and perhaps a bit of risk. Holly Bull, CEO of The Center for Interim Programs, specializes in helping all-age folks find the life/career they seek via the most bizarre sabbaticals. Among her clients are former doctors who have studied stone masonry and shamanistic healing. Other professionals have tried working at a wolf sanctuary in northern Canada or apprenticed under a mural painter in Mexico.

While such sabbaticals may not hold each seeker's personal ideal career, it does take that person out of his current milieu and provide a chance to examine what he truly wants out of life. Bull's services are excellent; however, you can just as well forge your own. Next time you read of a fascinating cabinet maker or dog sled racer, take the initiative. Call them up and see if they would like a volunteer intern. You'll only regret it if you don't call.

✳ **Selection Process.** As Ms. Bull puts it, "Most people back into their careers, seeking work from the wrong way around. They complete some given course of study, then list their salable skills and ask 'who will have me?'"

Instead, why not stare into your psychic mirror and ask, "What do I most want to do?" Then go out and gain the training it demands. There is a codicil to this method. Be sure to dose in a bit of time and reality into this dream-job formula. Do you have the time, free cash, and emotional stamina to carry you through the two decades of training to fulfill your fantasy of becoming a brain surgeon?

ATTITUDE ADJUSTMENT. Fantasize. Forget all the career paths and strictures you have been taught by elders so wise. Take that blend of skills and desires, and try to generate some different, oddball ways to apply them. Be prepared to shed traditional expectations of success for a more personal job fulfillment. Not easy, but definitely more satisfying.

BLUNDERS TO AVOID. Don't over commit. Don't let this moment's career passion plan out your whole life. Occupations are temporary. Dreaming to become a marine biologist, Ms. Bull once took a summer apprenticeship in a marine lab, an experience she utterly loathed. Fortunately, she had an exit strategy after this first-taste, trial job. So should you.

TIPS & TASKS. Look at your career. Ask yourself if you are living and laboring according to someone else's values. Is there another branch of your line of work that might offer better rewards? If so, could you use a sabbatical or some gap time to reassess? **BB**

Stop Chasing Symbols

Malcolm Forbes – Financier, Publisher

Too many of us mistakenly yearn for the symbol instead of our real goal. And that plants the seeds of lifelong dissatisfaction. All of us have been carefully taught what's important. Parents, teachers, bosses, and peers have explained it all over and over, each reinforcing each. Then one day, hopefully sooner than later, we individually wake to the notion that "their" importance might just not be ours.

The less inventive and more angry among us rage against the whole system of business. They feel pushed and manipulated. Like the war protester who would burn the Constitution after realizing the foolishness of one particular war, such folks sour on their whole career and everyone around it.

Truth is, it's not that parents, peers, or the system are corrupt. They merely are seeking simple yardsticks for comparing one person with another. And unlike you, these outside appraisers have access to only quantitative tools – size of salary or office, profits, output, corporate rank, overall wealth, or the number of people "under" you. While these methods of measurement are quick and easy to apply, they tend to be woefully misleading.

The real achievements and satisfactions, as you alone sense them, are what make up the qualitative success of your business career. What compares with that exhileration of watching your own creation unfold and come to market? Society and peers are powerless to bestow this kind of qualitative success upon you, so instead they slather on you the only things they have – success symbols. No one is recommending that you turn down the promotion, pay raise, or corner office. Just see it for what it is, and don't mistake it for your real goal.

✳ **Your Success vs. Theirs.** Shortly before his death in 1990, leading financier and publisher Malcolm Forbes, standing in the company of several others of the nation's wealthiest, was accosted by a reporter. "You gentlemen hold such an immense power," he burbled at Forbes. "Does the extent of that power ever dawn on you when you all get together?"

With great patience Forbes responded, "I cannot speak for others, but what concerns me most – what is most on my mind when we gather is the success of my own current project, and how in the world I am going to make it happen."

Forbes was basically stating that successful people of business place their greatest efforts and thoughts behind the creation and building of their enterprise. Let the outside symbols of wealth and supposed power fall where they may.

This past decade, American business has witnessed a tragic failure of faith and efficacy largely due to individuals chasing the shadowy symbols of success. Money and numbers, which investors ideally should be using as a way of keeping score, shifted to become the goal in themselves. Everything from solid financial products to personal character was sacrificed on the altar of quarterly projections alone. Hopefully, from this faith and fiscal failure, we will learn to place less trust in other people's yardsticks, be they a larger house or supposedly larger interest points.

✳ **Company as Product.** We live in an era in which companies are cutting back on every offering from investment instruments to airline routes and coffee grinders. Entrenched in survival mode, companies draw in their horns to only the 10 percent most profitable lines. Such decisions do not abandon the true creative spirit of business which benefits society and swells the chest of the creator. Business satisfaction need not be totally focused on presenting the best tangible product.

The company itself is a product benefiting society and individuals alike. For its owners and leaders, the company, more than its service, remains the primary product. And so, they make their choices. Few CEOs thrill to the sight of closed factory doors or empty work stations. Most are merely pruning as best they know how, to keep any crop at all yielding this year.

ATTITUDE ADJUSTMENT. Concentrate on pushing that next project through, with every ounce of oomph and smarts you possess. Then at day's end – and final completion – kick back, take a look. Feel your cares lift as the achievement shines. Truly, that is the unequaled exhilaration of business.

In religion, we witness that those who merely "love and do what they will" seem to be a whole lot happier in their faith than those who angst over the exact point symbolic wine turns to literal blood. So let it be with you. Focus on building the triumph visibly before you.

BLUNDERS TO AVOID. In your effort to avoid chasing symbols, please don't take on a holier-than-thou attitude. Of course you want more bucks, a promotion, and company growth. Steak tastes better than neck bones. So in your pursuit of the real goals, don't disparage the symbols that often come with them.

TIPS & TASKS. Look to your coworkers and review the rewards you are holding out for them. Are they a nice blend of tangibles and more personal fulfillment? BB

The Schedules You Keep

Pete Singer – Author, Philosopher, Animal Liberationist

It's a form of taking freedom's reins. Charting out your day and week does, indeed, help you get more done. It is also the surest snare into a performance rut whose high edges block the light of any grand vision, however lofty. With this caveat in mind, step back from your work time and think about breaking it down.

For many of us, there is a certain quota of items that must be completed each week, each day. Some of these are so obvious you scarcely need reminding. If your lab bench greets you each morning with a row of experiments, or your desk daily sports a roster of new clients awaiting your phone pitch, your routine seems fairly well laid out. But before you delete the calendar app from your smartphone, don't forget to look beyond mere quota, into longer-term, career enhancing ventures, and make time for them.

✳ **Stepping Back.** These pre-ordained quotas are part of the day – perhaps the major part. But beware of letting them become the entire day. Don't just ask yourself, "What do I gotta do tomorrow?" Instead, pause and consider. "What do I need to execute to make a satisfying life tomorrow – this week, perhaps even this month?" When you at last ease into that comfortable chair before the fire and contemplatively swirl a bit of your favorite reward in a glass, what accomplishments and labors will provide you a contented weariness?

Pondering briefly these last questions leads you beyond days of merely putting out workplace fires. A very wise Scottish chiropractor in Glasgow once outlined my therapy with the words, "Don't think of these as exercises, I want you to make them habits, frequently repeated at odd moments, throughout the day."

Throughout this volume flow scores of such short-time habits aimed at life and job enrichment. The maintenance person who develops

8

the discipline to scribble and sign a note of thanks or occasional organizing suggestion, not only connects with her clients, but promotes herself in an impressive, human way. The software technician who slates the time to call customers or fellow techies about new updates, achieves the same.

※ **Creating the List.** "Lists are wonderful," insists best-selling author and philosopher Peter Singer. "No line I write is so thrilling as the one drawn through a completed task on my chore list." However, it's best to create your epic "To Do" schedule at day's end or during more reflective moments. Nothing is so daunting as enumerating the upcoming hourly grind when you first settle into the office.

Begin, of course, with the stones in the river of your day: lunch with the client at 12:30, taking your son to basketball at 3:15, etc. Then, with little regard to the actual number of remaining hours, fill in things you would like to accomplish or labor upon. This includes the quotas, the business-bettering habits, and all other parts of your life. You might also note what would be the best time, mentally and generally, for you to attack each task. Our culture's entirely artificial separation from cash-producing time ("work") and the day's other segment ("leisure") tends to box our time unproductively. Don't merely think outside this box – tear it up and claim the entire day as your own.

Remember also that our best laid schedules "oft' go awry," as poet Robert Burns put it. Explosive problems, sudden cell phone calls, demanding e-mails, and more than we ever planned will doubtless happen. Such is reality. Get ready to shift and reschedule.

※ **Priorities Please.** Once you've filled in the schedule river 'twixt the stones of appointments, set in order what you can reasonably expect to do that day, that week. Blend in your personal breaks, your sport or exercise, the calls to coworkers, the surprise call to your spouse. Schedule actual appointed times to consider difficult questions and decisions. Realize that this schedule or list is an ongoing guide, not a chore list that must be completed by the midnight deadline.

With practice, your written schedule will actually make plain on the page/screen what is sensible for you to undertake. You'll find where to comfortably draw the line each day and week. The list of task items may string down long, but selecting each task in order and doling it a generous time slot should actually free you from the frenzy of that long leering list. And don't forget every once in a while to rip that schedule up and head for some spontaneous outing— (This inspires a feeling of well being seconded only by crossing off achieved items.) Remember, you are more than your to-do list.

Finally, it frequently helps to keep a journal or calendar with your schedule. Tax auditors often accept such journals, and it provides you with an overall record of accomplishments. It also acts as a warning about burrowing yourself into that performance rut. If you've really done all your correspondence at the same hour daily, is that tradition or best practice? As always, it's your day.

ATTITUDE ADJUSTMENT. View your schedule as a method of more effectively bringing your many talents to light. The schedule is your tool – you are not its slave. For many folks, schedules present a wincing "should list" of chores that we – or someone – deems vital. Viewed this way, every item listed becomes onerous. "Darn, now I've got to squeeze in my birthday party at 7 p.m."

If you cannot fit in everything you feel is demanded of you, look at who is making the demand. If it is you, the quota may be unrealistic. If it is not you, take trust. God will wait patiently, and if others will not, ask them for a hand.

BLUNDERS TO AVOID. Schedules are not designed to impress – you or others. Don't strive to be busy, or look busy on paper. Little benefit lies in bustling.

Don't forget to build in a realistic fudge factor. Everything takes more time than it should. Count on it. If you actually end up ahead of schedule, then treat yourself or use this windfall moment to employ one of your enrichment habits.

TIPS & TASKS. Be sure to assess periodically. Review your progress and see if your days are spaced to allow for maximum productivity and personal satisfaction.

Your schedule recording system must be one that suits you individually. Commercial planners and calendars may work well for a lot of people – but what do you need to keep you aware of the achievements behind and ahead? **BB**

Boiling It Down

Dr. Stephen Payne – CEO, Leadership Strategies, Inc.
Alan S.W. Dowie – Managerial Consultant

One clothing company's "Use of Logo" manual slaps down on the desk at 270 pages (a real manual.) Another company – a startup – has distilled its business plan to a mere 240-page yawner guaranteed to set any venture capitalist into a soporific stupor.

In an era in which words are processed, not written, 'tis only natural to churn them out like butter – the more the better. Unfortunately, writing more is seldom better. Concise writing demands precise thought, while unbridled verbiage often replaces thought, leaving the true goal undefined in the writer's mind.

The title *Manage Your World on One Page* by Dr. Stephen G. Payne and Alan S.W. Dowie pretty much says it all. Its authors assert rightly that if you cannot boil down to a single page your vision and the process for achieving it, then you just have not yet thought it through properly. Business ventures must be focused and clear to everyone involved if they are going to succeed.

☀ **Logical Steps.** The Payne/Dowie paradigm begins at page-top with a Vision – that place you want to be. This vision may be an expanding, profitable business, or becoming a respected, successful, satisfied individual. From there lead lines extend the pyramid down the page to a few logical Goals, Strategies for approaching each, and Tactics for achieving them.

One sweet feature in this planning page is the Measurement Step. Life is never a straight, unhindered march toward our envisioned objective. Throughout any plan, assessment of progress affords leaders opportunities to reset methods or goals for better achievement.

Taking such an approach for any business project makes the entire effort readily readable and comprehensible for all team members. Individual action plans are more easily divided, whether applied to a single task or a company as a whole.

✸ **You on One Page.** The first step is the toughest: your idealized Vision. Sit yourself down, alone and undistracted. Think deeply and consider your very individual pursuit of happiness. What three or four adjectives describe the person you want to be. Beware of falling into other people's goals for you. Also, reach for the true vision. Don't get caught up with building a boat when your true goal is to sail across the lake. For example, we all want money. But ask yourself, is obtaining wealth merely a method of achieving freedom, security, or perhaps it's a yardstick indicating success?

With an honest Vision of yourself firmly fixed, you may forge the goals that lead toward it. Items like a rich family life; emotional, mental and physical balance; career success and satisfaction and continual intellectual and educational growth might blend into the mix. It's your life. The choices are yours. Beneath each of these goals, list a couple of critical strategies, a few more specific tactics and disciplines.

Finally, at the page bottom, write a date for your plan's review, e.g., every four months. Mark the dates on your calendar.

The whole trick of actually writing out your life's plan is that it forces a great deal of focus and a great deal of thought. Allot yourself the time for this most valuable, life-motivating plan of action.

ATTITUDE ADJUSTMENT. Focus on your own vision. You were put here to eat life up with a spoon. Trouble is, most of us get stuck on one tasty dish or get distracted by each new item on the menu. You have been at the table long enough to consider what you really want. Admittedly, this complete freedom to select what you seek is a bit daunting. But take it, and don't let others decide for you.

Also, realize that you honestly will probably never arrive at some idealized state of fulfillment. (The real joy is in the voyage, anyway.) But you definitely will have a better shot if you set an exact target and carefully, deliberately take aim.

BLUNDERS TO AVOID. Write your own life plan first, before beginning with any business plan. Business is only a fraction of your greater life. Let your plan serve as a motivator. If you lace it with unrealistic goals and targets, it will petrify your efforts. Also, make the process enjoyable. The real happiness comes from the pursuit.

TIPS & TASKS. Your personal plan is your own, and naturally demands sole authorship. Yet for business one-pagers, get everyone involved in the creation. Select one author, but make sure everyone has their input. **BB**

Hard Work

It's required, but not all sufficient. It's no guarantee. Enough said.

TIPS & TASKS. Check yourself at day's end. Feeling exhausted does not necessarily mean you have worked hard. Make sure your precious store of energy has been smartly directed, and be ready to tweak your routine to expend it more effectively. **BB**

"John must be working hard. Look how exhausted he is."

The Parker House Rule

Ken Parker – President, Atlantic City Electric
Benjamin Zander – Symphonic Conductor, Motivational Speaker

Ken Parker is the stuff of which legends are made. In 1986 he entered the gate of Atlantic City Electric to take his first full time job – cutting the company's lawns. 18 years later, Mr. Parker perched himself on the edge of a soft leather chair after taking on the title of Atlantic City Electric's new president. Along the way, this African-American Jersey boy earned his Bachelor's from Delaware State University – the first ever in his entire family to graduate, or even attend, college.

When he casually mentioned his story a few years ago, I frankly couldn't believe it. I kept thinking, somebody's making this guy up. Such Horatio Alger tales aren't for real nowadays. But President Parker is very real, very, very bright, and very personable.

When asked the obvious question, Parker replied, "From the very start, I saw each assignment as an opportunity. I did every job they gave me as well as I possibly could and made myself the logical choice to move up." Sounds reasonable, if not terribly revolutionary. But then he added his personal Parker Success Touch.

✳ **Ask & See Rule.** "When first handed a situation, I would go around to everybody who was connected or in any way touched by this job and ask them what they wanted from me. I listened and wrote that down." Ken Parker formed his idea of a new job's requirements partially based on his own common sense, but equally on the expectations and needs of all involved. Parker did more than take responsibility after the fact – he foresaw the responsibility from people's viewpoints and adjusted his plan of action accordingly.

Will following this method land you in the president's chair? Unless you live in a Gilbert and Sullivan fable, probably not. Parker is one of those uniquely talented individuals. But his achievement certainly stands as proof of his method.

ATTITUDE ADJUSTMENT. View your current situation as a launching pad for all your potential. If you do not want to be seen as a human cog filling a job slot, don't treat your job like a disconnected slot. While still remaining in the real world, view yourself as an individual filled with a strong capacity to aid your company's productivity flow. This is what famed symphonic conductor and motivational expert Benjamin Zander calls *The Art of Possibility*. Ken Parker's Ask-and-See rule is simply a very practical way of bringing those possibilities to mind and checking to make sure they are indeed possible.

BLUNDERS TO AVOID. Ever wonder "What more do they want? I've done everything the job description asks of me."? If so, be prepared for about a C+ job review. Job descriptions cannot reveal all, and coworkers usually will not reveal all that is optimally required. 'Tis up to you to find out.

TIPS & TASKS. Try Parker's technique. Then chart your success in your own eyes and in the estimation of your coworkers. **BB**

As Others See Us

Janet Cargill – Image Consultant, Author

1. What sort of image do you want to convey to those around you?
2. What sort of image do you need to convey?

Take a moment. These two answers should differ. #1's answer might include adjectives like generous, sexy, admirable, good hearted... On the other hand, to be effective at work, you might answer #2 with e.g., authoritative, clever, competent, capable, open, a font of ideas, follows through... All of these positive perceptions – and negative ones as well – lie bundled in your image.

Your business image is a selection short cut that can place you where you want to be – or lock you in a glass cell. The right image is well worth crafting. Renowned personal consultant Janet Cargill has helped hundreds of business men and women create the image they require. In her book *Look Damn Good*, she teaches that image begins from within. It is a matter of letting your best self blossom and be seen by others undistracted. Your image need never be phony. Rather it should be a symbol to others of the strengths they may expect – and a private code of what you strive to be.

✳ **Crafting Tools.** Humans are perceptive. They see it all – clothes, posture, gait, language, expression – the entire package. Thus, consider all these things and get a little help in presenting them.

Daily, get a check from your roommate/partner; and be specific. "Does this make me look powerful, Jim?" Then listen when Jim tells you that turning your shirt right side out might augment the sought-after effect. Likewise, try out your general, informal greeting on Jim first. Ask him what your verbal tone conveys.

A one-time session with the right image consultant may prove well worth the investment. Color consultants who match skin tones with enhancing shades have stunningly made over many women. Most men need some sort of haberdasher to restrain them from reaching for that safety orange tie when interviewing. For most of us, an hour or two with a registered consultant is guaranteed to reveal, and correct, much. (Visit the Association of Image Consultant's International at www.aici.org.)

Finally, for the many of us who do not speak and write the King's English, a speech/presentation coach can be a career maker. It may seem unfair, but strong accents are a true business hindrance, particularly within the American community. Many public libraries offer enjoyable, mentored English conversation groups or can link you with free private tutors. Even if you are totally techie, your professional career will soar in direct correlation to your English skills. Make the investment.

Other tools in the quiver might include a good grooming kit. (Men – make sure it has a nose/ear/eyebrow hair trimmer.) Keep that kit and a hand-size mirror for the office for checking yourself occasionally. Ask your hair stylist. These are not effeminate fripperies. They are effectiveness tools. Abraham Lincoln once took down an opposing congressman and destroyed his entire speech by distracting everyone's attention to the man's unsightly, untrimmed eyebrows. A simple set of scissors or nose tissue might save your speech from that congressman's fate.

✳ **Radiating "The Look."** There is a difference between being well dressed and formally dressed. Sometimes an outfit upgrade may entail going from dress or sport coat to a suit. But gaze about your office and clients. Instead of increasing in formality, maybe having custom tailored, always clean, pressed, and color coordinated outfits is the better clothing upgrade. Remember, under dressing indicates you don't value those in front of you. Over dressing implies that you are expert at, well, just dressing formally. Both mask your business expertise.

Whatever the look, make it yours. "Anna" was a public speaker in whom Janet Cargill could find no appearance flaws. Shoes shined, beautifully fitting suits, coordinated blouses, she spoke with a carefully modulated tone which released all the right phrases. So where, in all this crafted image, was Anna? She wasn't letting her inside out. Her image shouted insecurely, "this should make them like me."

No one is suggesting Anna scuff up her shoes. But accounting executive Dave Geer adds a subtle touch of image individuality that instantly sets him apart. "As a kid, I always loved Taz, the cartoon Tasmanian Devil," says Geer. "I liked his action and wild whirling style." Not bad business traits, and fun. Today, Dave's shirts, and many ties, in faint but noticeable embroidery, show Taz kicking up his stuff. A symbol of what clients might expect from Mr. Geer.

As mentioned, gait, posture, facial expressions are all natural reflections of the inner self you want imaged abroad. Some of these, such as your smile and posture may be enhanced with practice, without becoming artificial. Again, you want the individual touch. Appearing open and pleasant natured most of the time is a good thing. Being always that way is bland. The ability to affect brief individual flashes of anger, compassion, and downright stubbornness makes your overall emotional backdrop seem real. Also, these sudden switches become more poignant because of the variety.

ATTITUDE ADJUSTMENT. Realize that you probably are not what you seem to others. Metaphorically (and perhaps literally) stand naked before the mirror and realize your many beauties and assets. Learn to see the many admirable facets of your reflected self.

BLUNDERS TO AVOID. Don't concentrate on the outside. Begin from within and think what outer, visible signs will best set this off. Don't be blind to your "audience" of coworkers. Yet don't become wholly persuaded by your perceptions of their values.

Don't be cheap in crafting your image. Open the pocketbook and spend to make yourself look good. Yet please refrain from telling people how much your clothes cost. The image that conveys, you do not want.

TIPS & TASKS. Recall times when you have been particularly well received. What was your tone? How did you look? What were you wearing?

Consider "costuming". One writer I know sold an article to a women's magazine publisher about the women in Zimbabwe because he came straight from the airport and looked appropriately grubby enough to have spent some months in Zimbabwe. Dressing to impress sometimes works. **BB**

Taming the Brain

Dr. Phil Nuernberger – Consultant, Author, **Strong and Fearless**

Sometimes our big fat brains get us into trouble. They just won't sit still and let us direct them.

Contrast our species, for a moment, with the humble, yet mainly successful woodchuck – a decisive beast who achieves most of his enterprises. Come after a woodchuck with a shovel and he will flee your garden fast as his pudgy legs will take him. Get too close, and he will turn flight to fight, rising on his hind legs and giving the attack his best shot – not vain or heroic, merely his best odds in that tight spot. Our woodchuck eats when he's hungry, drinks when he's dry, and seasonally finds some attractive ball of fur and makes more little woodchucks.

His human counterpart, however, after long and careful assessment, brushes instinct aside and flees when he should fight, fights when he should flee. When he's hungry and dry, his brain feeds him a diet of warnings and dread. The attractive woman leads him less often into mating and most often into paroxysms of angst-ridden petrification, with a whispering brain telling him, "what if...". Dr. Phil Nuernberger, explains this ebb and flow of angst to his Wharton Business School classes as "mind chatter." Our minds are enormous, unceasing engines that respond to every stimulus and siphon our thought onto an endless succession of tangents. Creatively, this is magnificent. It is this exquisite mental force that fills our cell phones with 600 Apps, sets robots on Mars, and inspires timeless, soul-piercing writings like *Hamlet*.

Yet like any faucet, you don't want it running all the time. To clear and focus your mind, Nuernberger suggests a form of Tantric meditation. There exist many effective, popular meditative styles, of course, but there are some basics that can be applied:

1. When totally alone, with some free minutes open to you, make yourself perfectly comfortable. Lie down on a floor with a small head pillow, arms spread. Using your diaphragm, breathe in through your nose and exhale in normal, regular breaths. Make sure these are belly breaths – that is, your stomach, not your chest should be rising and falling. Then from top to bottom, give yourself a brief relaxation check. Is your jaw relaxed? Arms? Shoulders? Feet? Toes? Once physically relaxed, focus your attention strictly on your breath. Think only of the breathing in and out.

   Very likely, other thoughts will come into your head. That's natural. Simply do not pursue them. Think of them as bubbles rising up in your stream of consciousness and let them flow down river, unattached from you. Finally, envision a candle flame or star in your mind, just between the eyebrows. Keep breathing, normally, steadily, using belly breaths, inhaling and exhaling through your nose.

   Some teachers say that after such mental cleansing you may, in this state, focus on a specific problem. Others say to gently come out of this mood and find yourself fresh to face the world. The choice is yours.

2. In mid confusion. When coworkers are in your face and the mayhem of the business day surges all around you, you require some sort of abbreviated self-settling to avoid getting caught up in the frenzy.

Try practicing brief, momentary breathing exercises, just described, while sitting at your desk. Try to clear the mind, let extraneous thoughts flow down river. And in a few moments clear your mind, so your full, unhindered resources will lead you to the best path of action.

ATTITUDE ADJUSTMENT. Work to build in pauses of consideration in all parts of your life. The most difficult aspect of business day meditation is getting rid of the artificial demand for speed. It is not how quickly you respond to a challenge that counts, but how well. Also be aware, meditation is not a break or vacation from stress and action. It is rather a redirecting of the mind to help you face it.

BLUNDERS TO AVOID. Don't worry about doing meditation "right." This is not one more exacting discipline. It is a focusing tool that, like all tools, must be adapted to you individually.

TIPS & TASKS. Try morning meditation when you first get up; it's the easiest time. Then make a habit of periodically meditating on the fly and settling yourself for action.

Also, meditation is not always a still life. The muse of mental focus may be courted while waxing the car, doing the dishes, or performing some simple, repetitive task. **BB**

Prowess – Not Fitness *A Word About the Body*

Frank Wells – CEO, The Walt Disney Company

You've doubtless heard it before. The body, mind, and spirit are exquisitely linked – each depends on the health of the other to function at its peak. Problem is, the human body is not designed for acquiring wealth. Tedious long hours laboring at the loom, behind the plow, on the assembly line, or hunched before the office desktop computer will ruin that magnificent, God-given biomachine. Nor can this destruction be entirely remedied by tacking on another hour at the gym. But cheer up. This does not mean that you must trade wealth for physical health.

After my wife and I had summited Mount Kilimanjaro and were trekking down the other side, we met Dick Bass. Pausing to huff and chat, he told us that he was heading up to the summit again to carve out a piece of obsidian which he would use as a marker for the grave of his friend, Frank Wells. He told me of how he and Wells had, as Rhodes scholars and chums at Oxford, decided upon a grand scheme to summit the highest mountain on every continent. Thus in 1954, climbing Kilimanjaro, Africa's highest peak, had provided one of their earliest adventures.

"Frank never made it to the actual summit of Everest," said Bass, "but you have to cut him some slack. After all, he was pretty busy as CEO of Disney." In 1994, businessman and inveterate heli-skier Frank Wells died when his helicopter crashed over Nevada's Ruby Mountains. No one can say this 62-year-old man did not live a full life.

I am not suggesting that balance in one's life comes only from leaping out of hovering aircraft onto steep virgin slopes and shrieking down some life-threatening run. But it makes me weep to witness rows of able bodies tending their mind-numbing treadmills in windowless rooms, with fatuous TV soaps flickering before their tired eyes. The business and life lesson exemplified so magnificently by Frank Wells is that great joy and satisfaction come from developing a positive prowess in some physical activity – rather than negatively plodding to fight off fat and stay fit.

❋ **Picking Your Play.** Your prowess may be as simple as weightlifting, or as complex as whitewater kayaking or ballet. It may be mild or extreme. The sole criterion is that you take joy in the process and look forward to your time doing it, not just achieving the goal. Actually, the greatest satisfaction comes from viewing your sport as a craft that you seek to ever improve.

Of course, if you opt for one of the more complex, logistically difficult activities, such as downhill skiing, you will want to spend those hours at the gym building up the necessary agility and leg muscles. It's all part of improving your prowess. And maintaining an overall fitness via calisthenics is a certainly nothing to be sneered at.

One little note, however. Studies continue to show that six 10-minute shots of physical exercise benefit the body far more than an hour of the same activity following an uninterrupted sedentary workday.

So whether you plan to hit the gym or not, do schedule physically active breaks. Get to know the stairwell in your building intimately. Get your eyes away from that oscillating computer screen at least once an hour, and work out a facial/eye area massage pattern that brings new blood to the situation. It's all part of bridging society's artificial chasm 'twixt work and play. Whether you earn your bread in a cube, in a truck, or in a home office, go creative and design a blend of physical stretches and activities during your time on the job.

If you're wondering what kind of activities to try you might start by hefting the enormous stack of physical activity guides available at your public library. If you can actually lift them all at once, you're probably already in good shape.

ATTITUDE ADJUSTMENT. Enter into the gates of physical exercise with "activity," rather than "regimen" in mind. Switch away from viewing training as an end in itself, and raise your aim to improving within your chosen sport.

BLUNDERS TO AVOID. Physical activity is not one more arena for self-flagellation. Do not push yourself toward over-lofty goals or punish yourself for not attaining them. There is no sensible link between failure and punishment. For heaven's sake have fun.

If you are jogging to conform your shape to someone else's ideal, you are destined to make the whole thing joyless. Run for your well-being and your happy feet.

TIPS & TASKS. Find a partner, someone with whom you may mutually enjoy and encourage in your sport. **BB**

Afterthoughts

❋ Time is your most precious, and most assaulted resource. Guard it well, above all. No one else will.

❋ Keep probing for reasons. Bring to light your real desire behind your actions and words. It will make your results much less surprising.

❋ Schedule time to think. A 5:15 p.m., Tuesday appointment with yourself to argue and consider sales strategy does wonders for self-direction.

❋ Strive not to be the ultimate business machine. To view yourself as such is a limiting insult to you, your potential, and your Creator.

❋ Seek out only one confidant and many mentors. More people want to help and encourage, than hurt you.

❋ Instead of stiffening your resolve, reach inside and determine why this task demands such will power. Modify from within.

❋ Enter business to please yourself first. Labor in ways and fields that bring you joy. If you don't believe in it, run, do not walk away.

❋ Tradition and best practices sometimes coincide, sometimes not. You have a brain to reason through the difference, and a strong enough will to convince others.

❋ Success and Satisfaction are insolubly linked. But Triumph and Disaster, as Kipling noted, are both impostors.

BB

CHAPTER 2

Becoming Aware

*"All these businessmen want to get into only one thing
– their customers' minds."*

Prelude

Facts stand plain before you. Understanding lies more subtly below the surface and must be teased out, one perception at a time. Knowledge and facts will strongly power your business ship forward. Understanding and awareness provide the helm.

This chapter discusses a few of the many elements working within your business environment. Keeping apprised of them and how they operate will give your working world a greater cohesion. Decisions will become clearer and more logical. Knowing, for example, the different expectations placed on men versus women in the business community may help make that "strange other gender's" actions less bewildering.

Several of this chapter's tactics deal with self-awareness. This is because you are the factor best primed to improve your situation. The blunders of immutable policy or the onslaught of daily persuaders are not likely to vanish in our lifetimes. However, the fuller your understanding of yourself, the greater your odds of responding flexibly and turning things to your advantage.

Who's Your Sugar Daddy?

Helen Gurley Brown – Former Editor-in-Chief, Cosmopolitan *Magazine*

Today's Lesson: Be mindful of the people using your product. However high your temporary perch, they put you there.

Helen Gurley Brown, legendary editor and guiding spirit of *Cosmopolitan* Magazine had just finished dancing with Chris Butler, Hearst Publication's then-Director of Circulation. As the music ended, she turned to Butler. "Look at them," said Brown, waving her hand across a floor of mostly male chief editors in whose honor the party was being given. "All of them have the same thing on their minds."

Knowing well Cosmo's content, as well as its editor's proclivities, Butler raised more than one eyebrow and awaited some Brownish quip such as "having an orgasm nook in their apartments on a budget." Instead, Ms. Brown sagely answered her question with "Every one of them is desperate to know what their readers want to read." Butler, himself a guiding force in publishing, often noted the wisdom of her words.

✳ **The Customer's Orbit.** The customer must ever remain the center of every business person's universe. This applies to everyone in the company, not just the sales force. (Editors, for example, are merely production managers in the publishing process, but their desire to burrow into the customer psyche was as great as any of Hearst's sales people's.) It is easy to get diverted from this focus. The product often tends to steal the show, and many an inventor can't see beyond it. Likewise, each person's piece in the process – distributing, purchasing, advertising, etc. – may work to shift attention away from the person who is actually using whatever you put out there. But you had better listen to and learn from that customer, because in the end, everything depends on him.

This does not mean that the customer is always right. "Give the customer what he wants," works fine, for awhile. Then, some world class innovator like Google or Apple will begin offering your customer something he never knew existed (or wanted), but now desperately craves. And you are history.

Also, as any veteran sales or marketing pro can tell you, customers don't always know, or say, what they want. Focus groups continually return surveys laden with fantasies, whimsy, and contradictory impossibilities that they truly don't (or wouldn't) care much for in the product. ("I only wish you would make a sports car with the trunk space and seat height of my SUV.") But though discerning is difficult, try to envision your company's customers, and keep them sitting on your shoulder as you perform the daily routine.

✳ **Client Respect.** The more you believe in your products or services, the higher your respect for those who purchase them. If you don't think much of what you are bringing to market, you'll probably view customers as foolish sheep whom you, with your considerable charm, herd into line to shear. Yet in truth, such a cynical client view reflects most poorly on the purveyor. None is so great a fool as he who knowingly stands behind shoddy or fraudulent merchandise.

Further, all of us hunger for true respect. And even the slowest witted customer senses in a flash whether he's being held in high regard, or being buttered by a con man. Count on it, you can't disguise contempt, but it's a small matter to instill yourself with some customer appreciation.

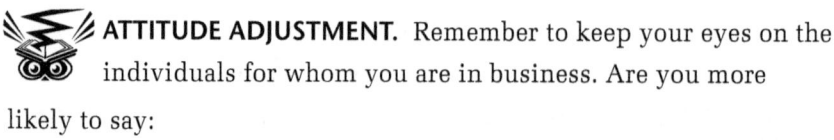 **ATTITUDE ADJUSTMENT.** Remember to keep your eyes on the individuals for whom you are in business. Are you more likely to say:

1. I am an importer of the very finest French and German wines.

OR

2. I am a purveyor of imported wines to select restaurateurs and sommeliers throughout the tri-state area.

Develop the mindset of **2.** and keep your focus on the person paying your bills.

BLUNDERS TO AVOID. Beware of flash trends and consumer whimsy. Do consider customer history, and employ a bit of common sense psychology in anticipating customer needs.

TIPS & TASKS. Establish a periodic schedule of check-in calls with customers and potential clients. Ask them how they like your firm, its products, its services, and its people. Ask for suggestions. Remember, these are not sales calls. Make sure the only thing discussed is a request for the client's opinion. And by the way, you do not have to be on the sales team to reach out and ask. **BB**

Demon Policy

Though practical sometimes, operating according to the gospel of labyrinthine company policy typically hobbles production and stifles human innovation. If you must set functioning policies, make them for things that positively unclog and encourage the work flow.

Good policy: It is our policy for sales people to report notable customer responses to marketing and product development directors.

Dumb policy: It has always been our policy always to have all sales personnel fill out the triplicate colored sheets after each customer encounter and send them to the sales manager's desk.

Each attempts the same goal. The former affords individual discretion, and provides inherent explanation for the action. It may even lead to the development of new products, services, and sales. The latter allows no individual judgment and makes the form filler wonder **a)** why he or she is doing this and **b)** what kind of idiot ordered this move.

ATTITUDE ADJUSTMENT. Examine your policies. Eliminate any rule or task that does not have an apparent, beneficial reason beyond mere policy. Such tasks only put a burr under the performer's saddle that hinders both his and the company's production.

TIPS & TASKS. Consider the work style of those to whom you assign policy-driven tasks. Perhaps there is another approach rather than asking numbers-crunching accountants to write onerous essays or burdening non-detail-oriented sales people with lengthy report forms. Strive to be a human dealing with humans. **BB**

Science – Art – and Magic

Stephan Schiffman – Author, **Cold Calling Techniques**
Mitch Schaefer – Trainer, Sandler Institute
Greg Williams – The Master Negotiator

Before you assign or undertake a task, 'tis best to know what it really demands.

Every business achievement falls along the continuum of process vs. performer. That is, how much of its success depends on the method followed, versus the individual performing it.

At one end stands pure science. Anyone can do it. If a Nobel laureate chemist, a shoe salesman, and a mischievous schoolgirl each follow the prescribed formula and mixes equal portions of charcoal, saltpeter, and sulfur, each will make workable gunpowder. Success lies intrinsically in the method.

On the other end stands pure art. Many people may wield identical brushes and paints. Each may employ the same method, but only Vincent can make a van Gogh. And only you – not Shakespeare – can make a memo that "sounds so just like you." It all hinges on the person.

Somewhere in between, and in most all business, lies magic. Here, achievement is brought to fruition by the gifted hands of the right individual working through the best possible process. Many people may learn the secret by which the Great Houdini mysteriously escaped his bonds. And while this secret formula is necessary to performing the magical escape, without the artistic skill of Harry Houdini, most of us would die padlocked in that straightjacket.

Toward which elements of the continuum do you want to focus your business endeavors? All three.

✷ **Mentoring the Magic.** Few people have honed the cold sales call to the precision format as expertly as Stephan Schiffman of DEI Sales Training Systems. His book *Cold Calling Techniques* is a business classic. Schiffman has dissected this daunting experience and produced a process that removes the terror and vastly increases the success rate. Likewise, the Sandler Sales Institute has packaged a host of adaptable techniques that have empowered such trainers as Mitch Schaefer who blends the Sandler method with his personal sales power. This passing on of techniques that have magically catapulted forward some stellar performer is a necessary part of all training.

Every executive should keep his antennae alert for top performers in any field, who may mentor the scientifically repeatable elements of their achievements. The burden here falls on the mentor to examine his success, and remove much of his own artful persona from the mix. He must seek to distill the pieces of his success which may be most easily adopted by others. Both the executive and the mentor must remember that the methods passed on are not carbon-copy, reproducible formulae. Each team member, after all, embraces his own artistic style that will turn the key his own way and undo the straightjacket's padlock. He may never be a Houdini, but he'll get the job done.

✷ **Science: Yes You Can.** Some boxes do not need thinking outside of. So it is with many business labors. By 1862, most modern armies knew that it took 12 men to effectively entrench a field artillery piece. By the mid-1920s the stress capabilities for most common building materials had long been time tested and recorded. The formulae had proven themselves worthily through time.

The trick comes in determining which methods of operation are based in experiment-proven science, and which are merely parts of hidebound, traditional policy. Perhaps knowing the difference takes a bit of the artist. But a little hand comes from the magic of professionalism.

There is no need to attribute mystical titles, excessive remuneration, or awe to those gurus who have conquered formidable niche business routines with a personal flair. Computers are not for wizards only – honest. Most legal documents may be interpreted by people who can read well. Most accounting methods, e.g., tax and payroll reporting, have been condensed to the one sure way that works. However, a good professional in these areas can move your operation rapidly through the cookbook formulae stage and on into higher levels of expertise.

✳ **The Savings of Art.** Sometimes, it is all about the individual. Not only the great personalities – the Gates, the Forbes, the Iacoccas – but those who just have the knack.

Greg Williams who rightly titles himself as "The Master Negotiator" is the man you want sitting at your side of the table during your next dispute. He has a vast arsenal of techniques, many of which may be found in his weekly online newsletter *Negotiation Tips*. But in the end, the whole body of these elements is so complex and interwoven that it just pays to set self-training aside and hire Williams – the artist.

ATTITUDE ADJUSTMENT. Review your varied business tasks and determine which demand art, science, or magic. This is more than a curious intellectual exercise, suitable for post-prandial theorizing. Realizing how much of each success may be credited to the process and how much to someone's own innate artistry allows you to repeat your triumphs and avoid future failures. It also can guide you into further sharpening personal skills and tweaking some processes.

BLUNDERS TO AVOID. Beware of labeling extremes. Pedestaling someone as a mystical wizard makes his or her achievements unobtainable and limits your own aspirations. Conversely, assuming that you may conquer any task once you can pry loose the right secret is simply not realistic. It leads you to ignore your unique personal talents and seduces you into spending a fortune on step-by-step self-help books, like this one.

TIPS & TASKS. Look through your organization and find one individual who just has that knack – whose techniques for success appear unrepeatable by anyone else. Can you name three traits or tools this person employs consistently? Would they work for you?

Finally, look at the mentoring you are doing and see how adaptable you have made it for another individual's use. **BB**

Only Everything They Need

Dan Conley – Founder, OnCall CFO, and of New Jersey Entrepreneurs Forum
Jack Welch – Former CEO, General Electric Corporation

It's not what you write or say. It's what you pause to consider beforehand.

Dan Conley is exasperated. Not a good sign if you are an entrepreneur. Dan is witnessing a startup CEO commit Death by PowerPoint before a group of venturists he hopes will fund him. Our CEO rhapsodizes about the wonders of his innovative product. (See very technical, exploded-model slides.) He carries on about how everyone will want to buy this marvelous gadget. (Note complex marketing chart and graph slides.)

This presenter is an entrepreneur Conley has chosen and coached for his select New Jersey Entrepreneurs Forum. He wouldn't be there unless his product and company were very worthy of investment. Finally, Conley can stand it no more.

"Get to the money." Dan interrupts out loud. "Tell 'em how much you need, what you are going to do with it, and how many customers it will buy." After an awkward silence, our flustered entrepreneur begins again, this time telling the venture capitalists what they need to hear.

Jack Welch, famously sharp-tongued former head of General Electric, was not nearly so gracious as Conley. "Gee Harry, you must have had a great fourth grade education," he would roar across a full assembly hall to some poor division head during his presentation. "You read those slides so well to all of us." Welch's motto (which he was no less loath to yell out) was "Unless you have something to say that gives value to everyone in this room, get off my stage."

✳ **What Are You Doing?** Business entails being busy – having a full day. Your time is precious. So is that of your colleagues. Whether you are making a formal presentation, whipping off a fast e-mail, or visiting a client, consider why you are making this effort. What do you really want to get across? Then, further consider what this individual needs to hear. Conley's entrepreneur did indeed need to provide a thorough and full explanation of what his company was producing and how they planned to sell it – eventually. But right now, the part that touched his venture capitalist audience was how much of their money did this guy want, to purchase what. Hook the listeners with that, and they may willingly invest more of their valuable time for added explanation.

Likewise, ask yourself, am I visiting this client merely as a knee-jerk response to having a new product upgrade? Or have I figured out some individual benefit that I want to concisely lay before her?

✳ **Why Are You Here?** This is the macro version of the more immediate question just discussed. Why are you in business? Whether employee or owner, what are your plans for this company? There are a couple of right answers to these questions.

1. You are in business to make money. You may have fallen in love with your product or service and think every soul on this terrestrial orb is panting for it. You may feel you've come across a way to make the world a much better place. And perhaps you have. But just remember, of the five individuals who simultaneously invented the telephone, we credit only Mr. Alexander Graham Bell – the man who benefitted us all by turning the telephone into a money-making business.

2. You aren't a business until you have customers. This is Conley's primary maxim (even before "Get to the money".) The entire aim of business must be to get something into a person's hands for which he or she willingly gives you cash. Seems obvious, but it's easy to let this foremost target slip away due to over-focusing on the product, or clinging to traditional processes.

Side note: Often, as is the case for many larger corporation owners and senior staff, the company and its stock become the product itself. Yet even here, the goal remains to concentrate on those customers investing their dollars in your entity.

ATTITUDE ADJUSTMENT. Get to the heart of the matter by using whatever mental preparation works for you. Before you speak or flip open your laptop, or fondle your smartphone screen, pause a moment and consider the point of your action. Then consider the person with whom you are connecting. Think about what he or she requires, and address that first.

BLUNDERS TO AVOID. Beware tradition. Acting or communicating as it has been ritually done seldom fits each individual situation. This does not mean that fixing periodic communication times and meetings is a bad thing. Just mentally establish what parts of this chat are really vital.

On the other hand, don't always become a "bottom-line speaker." It limits your thinking. Conley's entrepreneur should have addressed the money and its purpose at the outset. But he also needed to inform them (and show them that he knew) the full scope of his company.

TIPS & TASKS. Browse through the "Sent" box in your e-mail. Review how well your messages have gotten to heart of the matter, while still considering the goals of the recipients. Do you do make these considerations better or worse when speaking formally? Informally? **BB**

Business Education by Foot

A wealth of drama and valuable business insights await. And most of us stroll self-absorbedly by it every day. How much do you know about the people plying their trade all around you? How often do you take advantage of their knowledge?

My wife was the hospitalized patient. I was the doting spouse, traipsing back and forth, encountering hoteliers and hammer slingers, surgeons bustling in, and orderlies wheeling their charges out. The business community splayed wide before me, as it does for most people on their daily route to work.

Would it be worth my while to pause and, on the fly, inquire into the vagaries of these people's jobs? The bounty of practical knowledge this garnered overwhelmed me.

✳ **Look for Pain.** In the elevator. "Off to the surgery?" I inquired. He nodded slightly. (Surgeons are not a markedly chatty lot.) "It always struck me that the number of operations they heap on you guys is immense," I kept on. "Do you get some sort of comedown break? I know I'd find such task shifting really tough."

I had unleashed the floodgate. This fellow was feeling overworked, over pressured and here, for once, was one of the laity who at least had a glimmer of his side of the equation. Within the next five floors, he gave me an exquisite capsule of his profession's crush, blended with some rather surprising personal revelations that I'll leave unsaid here.

Not everyone instantly warms to the overture of a stranger, even one admiring their work. But if you can train yourself to see at least one challenge this person may face in performing his job, the connection will be made. Try to stick with just one job hurdle, not the entire career. Instead of commenting to the professional mediator, "Boy, I'll bet it's tough transforming adversaries into fellow problem solvers in your work," try, "It must be tough to keep your own objectivity, sometimes." The second comment offers a smaller chunk for him to chew and respond to.

✳ **Seek and Assess.** You, as witness to the lady's labor behind the counter, offer a little appreciation and interested inquiry. She, in turn, will inadvertently provide you with a little expertise or wisdom. It's more than a greeting. This little midstream pause forges a brief, unexpected human connection and makes a mutually beneficial trade.

Basically simple, but it requires some thought. To the fellow swabbing the washroom, you might remark, "Boy, this place looks spotless. Say, how many of these things are you able to cover in a day?" With a few words you have validated this man's labor and thus his existence. You have ignited a touch of pride by recognizing his work. But it doesn't fall dead with a gratifying compliment. The immediate next sentence shows interest from an appreciative source.

You are the novice seeking this master's knowledge. Of course he will answer you and, with a little luck, provide more maintenance info than you ever wanted to know. You, meanwhile, walk away with a little negotiating leverage when it comes to hiring a cleaning service or dealing with your office landlord, or perhaps just a relatable story. Imagine what you might learn from the construction crew or the techie on the train with his laptop.

"Undercover Boss" is a television show currently soaring in the ratings. Here, various incognito CEOs slip in amongst their company's rank and file and share their challenges. While these episodes may make high jinx entertainment, they represent what all owners and leaders should be doing constantly. If a CEO has not personally kept communicating with his workers and learned the many problems they overcome, he is cheating his board and shareholders. It should not take the enticement of a TV appearance to know your staff.

In time, this hobby will become a habit, and you will find yourself recognizing unnoticed people performing pieces of business you never knew existed. By lifting your nose out of the financial pages and examining the real world, you will finally gain a more complete picture. As your inquiries lay bare the complex interweavings of the commercial realm's fabric, you may begin to place your own labors in the larger human perspective. Also, you are casting an awful lot of sunshine to lot of people that may just come back to shine your way.

ATTITUDE ADJUSTMENTS. Open yourself to the masteries of those around you. Snobbery is a comfy blanket in which we cozily wrap ourselves in the assurance that our success springs only from our own merit, not good luck. But remember, the key to wisdom is to never consider the source. Many of those unnoticed business people you encounter, with smaller salaries and less formal education than you, still hold marvelous insights. Doff the blanket. Get over it and introduce yourself to the human race.

BLUNDERS TO AVOID. Watch your tone. Avoid sounding condescending to those you might deem of lower station, or rapturously over-complimenting those you deem above. The whole point of this meeting is to establish a connection of equals – fellow to fellow. Speak the same words you would use to invite a buddy for beer.

TIPS & TASKS. Stepping up to strangers involved in work fills most of us with a wincing dread. Obviously, pick your times. It's not wise to interrupt a welder when his torch is lit. You may find it easier to make your initial appreciative remark out loud, to no one in particular, rather than addressing it directly to the working individual. As a start, try conversing with that person who sells you your daily paper.

As you walk into your workplace, quickly tabulate how many different jobs it takes to make this building function. Count the number of jobs you see along the street that literally make your day possible. Calculate the approximate expense for operating the building or that section of town. Feel gratitude, if you want, but this is an exercise in awareness. A few such calisthenics will greatly aid you in understanding and planning your own project's strategy. **BB**

When to Turn Off the Lights

Sam Walton – Founder, Walmart Stores

"When Sam Walton opened up his Walton's Five and Dime near my store in Bentonville (Arkansas), he found a source for toiletries that was a full 50 percent below anyone else. So, darn near every night Sam would drive the five hours round trip to stock up and sell them at this rock bottom price in his store. I also knew of this source, but I just decided I didn't want to live that way. So I guess that's why he's Sam Walton, and I'm not." –*John Dunham, owner,* Sterling Store, *competitor of Sam Walton, 1961.*

Test yourself. What is your instinctive, gut reaction after reading this tale about America's wealthiest retailer? If you felt a wave of personal inferiority or career regret, then, my friend, you are in the majority – and you have not quite passed. You have yet to determine the appropriate extent of devotion to business that brings your life satisfaction. And the time to do that is now.

For generations, business achievement has stood as one of the few status yardsticks in much of our modern culture. It is the only real way to enter America's nobility. Admittedly, this is not a bad thing. Making one's mark by building a societally contributing business serves far better than bloodletting one's way to the top through rapacious military adventures.

However, the commonly held method of obtaining such success has become a somewhat flawed mythology. Look at Sam Walton, the parable preaches. He rose from store clerk to an unequaled Emperor of Retail by a ruthless, monomaniacal devotion to business. That, my son, is the only way to succeed. But in truth, one myth does not fit all.

* **Smart vs. Slavish.** This little folk tale reveals more about Mr. Walton than his frightening fixation with commerce. First, it shows he was ever on the prowl for new suppliers. Wise idea. It further demonstrates Walton was true to his company's niche. Also sharp. He had designed his first store, a Ben Franklin franchise, for strictly the lowest-price retail market. The trek for cheap toiletries, thus, made sense. He was working hard and smart.

Was Walton's life of 18-hour business blitzkrieg days satisfying for him? Did the more relaxed life suit Walton's competitor who told this tale? That's of no concern to you, really. Your job is to discern where your own fulfillment level lies. No one is denigrating hard work or long hours. Few things better your odds of success more than these. But don't get caught up in other people's models. Success comes from a blend of many paths and efforts. Some will slide into wealth by selling Pet Rocks. Others will labor long years to creating a complex software package. The results of business are elusive and vastly unfair, so you had better love the daily work.

Society dangles the carrot of status to those who follow the Walton model. Meanwhile others insist on living a "balanced life" – whatever that is. Ignore them all. Work as your business demands and as your sense of fulfillment dictates. Then turn off the light, lock the door, and go pump iron, heft a cognac, or kiss a lover.

ATTITUDE ADJUSTMENT. Forget the impostors of "success" and "failure." Let your passion for the job dictate your devotion and the number of frantic hours you expend over it.

Also, realize and accept, however grudgingly, that some really lazy idiots will find tangible success far above yours. It has happened to everyone before. It will happen to you. You are not alone. In truth, it is quite unlikely that more than one percent of those in business will ever make it into business's top one percent. Hard work, enterprise, cleverness, ability – all the virtues – are constantly thwarted, or aided, by luck.

BLUNDERS TO AVOID. Don't prod yourself – particularly with other people's spurs. Let your natural love of achievement fuel your ambition. If that is not happening in your workplace, maybe it's time to jump toward something more fulfilling.

Also, don't box your life. Yes, you do need to measure out your dedication to business and all the emotional commitments of your days. You do need to allot certain hours of time. But beware of boxing your mind and spirit into a separate mode for each activity. Instead follow the heart's lead and let thoughts and feelings flow as they will through the day.

TIPS & TASKS. Write down a list of the variables in your business over which you hold absolutely no control. Put an X by the items which are likely to continue for awhile. Secondly, instead of bemoaning the odds stacked against you, make another list, jotting down a few of your recent successes. Then stand amazed at your achievements, particularly in the face of all those uncontrollable obstacles that you've overcome. **BB**

Men Tote Trunks/Women Carry Purses

It's different for women in business than men. No. I am not about
to beat the aged and untrue drum of poor, poor pitiful womankind
struggling through a male-dominated realm in which all men are
rapacious sexists...etc., etc. Most all sensible folks know that no
behavior is universal and that it's sheer bigotry to lump all individuals
in a group as always believing "that way". Enough said.

A far greater anchor to business success than one's gender is the
baggage of expectations most newcomers drag into the halls of
commerce and industry. And certainly though every person's load
is unique, society has, and still does, place different pressures on
gentlemen and ladies. We point these out not to categorize, but rather
to help the readers discern their own parcel of what others expect of
them, and how to deal with these views.

As mentioned in the previous section, business has long been one of
the few status yardsticks in our modern culture. Historically, for men,
achieving in business stood as a mark of masculinity, one's ability
to provide, and gain rank. For many it has proven a powerful
aphrodisiac, able to o'erleap youth and good looks. Though perhaps
less blatantly stated today, these rewards are still held before the noses
of eager men, both young and old. One becomes expected to rise in his
trade, since his whole being depends on it.

For women coming full force into the workplace over the last three
decades, a new image has been carved. The symbols may be differently
tailored, but the promise of status remains just as sure. The working
woman who forges a certain business position may expect a new
respect within all levels of her community. She is taken seriously and,
quite often, is seen as admirably serious. The woman has her own
independence through income. And, she is "Busy, Busy, Busy" –
apparently a noble goal for both men and women. Again, the woman's

self-esteem hangs on the performance expected of her. She thinks better of herself when she fits society's bill.

Many mutual-gender pressures exist for the business novice, but perhaps none so detrimental as the belief that anyone can scale the summit, and everyone should. With enough gumption, guts, and talent, you too can dwell in the rarefied air of Bill Gates and Warren Buffett. And if you aren't sitting in their palaces of power, my business friend, you have failed.

The problem with this ultimate achievement fantasy is that it serves to petrify, rather than spur, ambition. We are justifiably overwhelmed at how high the corporate ladder rises – at how small our firm's profits compare with the "big players."

Expectations in themselves, of course, are not bad, nor are any of the promises just listed. But it is important to examine what you believe others expect of you and what you may realistically expect from your career. If you can ignite your ambition by the joy of business creations, rather than focusing on some vague success ladder, you are more likely to catch the real excitement.

ATTITUDE ADJUSTMENT. Throw away the yardstick. Rather than vowing to make your first million by age 25 or vice-president by next year, strive to develop your first product or increase market share by next fiscal year. Work to ignore the success landmarks of others. View any benefits accompanying your various achievements for what they are – perks.

BLUNDERS TO AVOID. Beware of tangling your business status with your identity. You are "Sheila" who also happens to serve as vice-president of Acme Software. Not the reverse.

TIPS & TASKS. Make a list of those people most influential in your life. Beside each name, list what you think he or she expects from you in your career. Review the list once and see if this is an honest assessment of their expectations. Review it again and see if these expectations are realistic for you. **BB**

Word Victims

An entire conspiracy of propaganda lurks at every turn – verbal hooks at the ready – striving desperately to twist you to somebody else's will. It has been estimated that the average American (whoever she is) daily faces over 2000 advertisements. Add to these cash-extraction persuaders the messages urging us to think, behave, believe, like, dislike, view, and listen in a way that best benefits some other person or group.

Americans are the best, bar none, at this propaganda seduction, and it has played a key factor in our business supremacy. The old maxim holds true, that when the Germans want to sell a car to the Japanese, they call Americans to advertise it. But it is vital that the independent business person, seeking to employ his thoughts freely, be aware of those many hidden persuaders that vie to nudge his own "original" ideas.

✳ **Masters of Seduction.** Some institutions are so historically expert that they have spread their persuasive ideals beyond their own group into the society at large. For millennia, the military's propaganda machine has been able to prop up people employed in the appallingly distasteful work of murdering their own species. Many religious leaders have, for an equal term, been able to entice their flocks into a host of unnatural acts ranging from abstinence to suicide.

Please note, we are launching no call for the disbandment of the military or religion. Soldiering has been the making of many a young person, providing him or her skills, financially remunerable expertise, and the ability to see through the fearful facade of rank and professionalism.

As for the benefits humankind has received from her religions – it is instantly terrifying to imagine a world without the gifts and good they continually bring.

This said, we invite you to examine the following definitions, stripped of their typical societal connotations. You do not have to agree with these definitions. That's the point. Neither do you have to agree with the definitions you have been taught.

Duty – The ongoing course of action one takes to fervently serve the will of another.

Code – One's personal guide for what seems the most productive and satisfying way. It may originate with the follower or have been sold to him by someone else.

Honor – An intangible feeling of self-worth achieved from obedience to duty or a code.

Devotion/Dedication – The avid, if unexamined, following of some plan or someone who often claims authority beyond himself, e.g., a deity, president, or individual of rank.

Scripture – An organization's code of words that someone else wants to convince you holds the final, unquestionable authority on a subject. Business likes the synonyms "document," "manual," and "paper."

You get the idea. A host of emotionally dripping words surround us, each designed to keep our free beliefs and actions on someone else's course.

ATTITUDE ADJUSTMENT. In business and out, join or shun a plan based on your own satisfaction first. You alone must be the sole guardian of what is best for you. Simply be aware that many individuals, and all groups of individuals, have plans for your time, energies, dollars, and beliefs. They seek to entice you to this way and that, primarily for their benefit, and only secondarily for yours.

BLUNDERS TO AVOID. Beware of rejecting any idea merely because its author is powerful. Cynicism sows seeds of personal havoc as great as any institution. We urge our children to brush their teeth, your wife urges you to lose 15 pounds, your priest urges you to lend others a helping hand. Not every person and group's wishes for you are destructive.

Also, avoid terrorizing yourself with conspiracy theories. If you come upon an institution that feeds its own greed while masquerading as a public benefactor, go ahead and lead your own unmasking crusade. But you will only haunt yourself by seeking plots hatching under every bed.

TIPS & TASKS. Take a look at how you typically persuade coworkers to accept an idea or take on a job. Ask yourself how much individual benefit you are affording these people for acting or adopting your recommendations. What is their reward? **BB**

Afterthoughts

⁕ Steer your ship by focusing on the swift, smooth, forward current you seek to follow – not the obstacles you wish to avoid.

⁕ If you can find any way to be asked, rather than openly tell about your business, by all means, employ it.

⁕ Catalog your prejudices – toward people, situations, things. Holding such judgments up to the harsh light of consciousness makes leashing them, or banishing them, easier.

⁕ The better you know yourself, the better you'll know your business. The two are inseparable.

⁕ Develop several single-sentence taglines about your job, company, and product. Make them lyrical, and above all memorable. And please, never cutesy.

⁕ Pretend, or perhaps, you actually are forming a top business team. What areas are you strong enough to handle by yourself? What jobs should you realistically hand over to professionals?

⁕ Learn the facts of a business by reading. Learn the truth about it by talking with its least-paid employees.

⁕ If you are finding fulfillment in your day's work, then your career is doing its job.

CHAPTER 3

Playing Profitably With Others

*If your listeners keep feigning a vibrating cell phone in their pocket,
it is probably time to be quiet and give them a chance to speak.*

Prelude

Business is a matter of dealing with people. That's part of what makes commerce so gratifying – and amusing. The very tangling of individual wills, histories, and desires when business folks meet presents a drama worthy of any stage.

Yet business interplay involves more than theatrical fiction. Real livelihoods are at stake here. The better you personally engage with people, the better your business will thrive. Count on it. The burden of developing these people-play abilities falls heavily on you alone. You cannot outsource these vital abilities. You cannot hide behind front men who claim magnificent "people skills." No one wants to conduct trade with unseen decision makers lurking in the background.

Intentionally or not, you are already your firm's spokesperson. You are also the foremost billboard for yourself as a business asset. The short list of techniques in this chapter should help you improve those valuable roles. Paying particular attention to this chapter's Attitude Adjustments will help make these techniques personally most effective. After all, sincerity, not show, is the number one rule of business engagement.

First Encounters

William Makepeace Thackery – Author
Mark Twain - Sage, Humorist, and Author

You have just encountered an individual of great potential. Through luck or strategy, you now are sitting across from that person who can enhance your career and business, or she is just some luminary who is beneficial to know.

Your first, instinctive reaction most typically is to?

1. Convince this power person through subtle, modest phrase insertions that he is conversing with an equal, i.e., let him know that you are every bit as good as he.

2. Do whatever it takes to develop a relationship with this person that may be continued, e.g., search out some common ground, and then suggest a future meeting.

3. Listen, awed by her rank and wisdom, and wait to scoop up some apple of knowledge or a connection that you can use.

4. Pause, find the precise time to bring up your need – how this person of power can serve you to your best advantage.

5. Grovelingly rain compliments upon her with, in the words of William Makepiece Thackery, "an obsequiousness that only a free born Englishman is capable of."

None of these gut reactions sounds particularly complimentary, and, when so worded, they aren't. But all of them are very, very human. We quite naturally want to rub up against people of power, and at the same time, we feel a bit threatened. It also only makes sense to seize the opportunity to make the most of a new connection.

The caveat here is to take note of your own typical gut reaction when meeting new people. Realize that this initial impulse will most likely translate into your first action in this person's presence. And frankly, first meetings with strangers are not necessarily a time to go with your gut. So cloak your naked desire in a gown of polite conversation. Act as one human chatting with another, and await results.

ATTITUDE ADJUSTMENT. Dredge up and consider your attitude towards individuals of power or potential to aid you. Do it before entering the social arena, (e.g., now would be a fine time). Examine these views. Both power and potential are generally illusory, so try to resculpt your image of such folks as, well, just folks. Choking down envy is never easy. When introduced to a person of notable rank, try inquiring about his family or some small, intricately difficult part of his job. It will keep both your mind and his off of the difference in position.

BLUNDERS TO AVOID. "Few men can endure success. Another man's I mean," noted Mark Twain. Obviously, shows of challenge or obsequious over-complimenting only indicate your most unattractive insecurities. (Guaranteed, the powerful don't feel threatening, so don't you feel threatened.) At the same time, don't rush the relationship. Business dealings, like friendships, require a certain settling-in courtship. People want to feel each other out. So don't strike and conquer.

Beware of focusing your conversation on this person's rank or prominent achievements.

TIPS & TASKS. Practice your approach. Plan out half a dozen ways of engaging individuals in conversation, with an eventual aim toward their benefiting you. Test your approaches out on strangers. Then keep track of their response. Be sure to choose a no-penalty place like a local pub or the commuter train, not a neighborhood party. Remember to treat each of these strangers as an individual of great potential – they may just be.

Make a great show of shutting off your hand-held device to imply the exceptional value of this encounter. **BB**

Balancing the Scales

Herb Ballinger – Managing Editor, **Boating Industry Magazine**
Teena Cahill – Director, Wisdom & Beyond, LLC

He arrived in the office somewhere between 7:00 and 7:30 a.m. Twelve hours later he trudged out, heading homeward on an hour-plus commute. Managing Editor Herb Ballinger was devoted to *Boating Industry Magazine* with a tacit passion that you don't see much any more. Somewhere around 4:30, Herb would begin to show signs of wear. It was understandable. I was just out of college as a *Boating Industry* assistant editor, and Herb was "really old" – perhaps 45.

But no matter how fatigued he was, about 15 minutes before the end of the business day, you would find Herb on the phone calling three people. To each one he would say "You know, I just came across a piece of information and I thought it might be of use to you...." He defended this ritual to me by explaining that all day long we writers and editors interviewed and essentially took information from people. If you unexpectedly gave some of it back at random occasions, you would, as Herb put it "balance the scales."

✳ **The Give-Back Discipline.** Like a pre-meal pause for grace or daily sit-ups done just after rising, setting aside a specific time for a reciprocal moment ensures it will get done. Regardless of what form your favors take, it's a good idea to keep an ongoing file of those who have helped you throughout that week and month. Not only does it allow you to target whom you call, it makes you aware of who is buttering your bread.

It may work out that a daily or even weekly appointed time of giving back simply won't fit your schedule. Fine. Just keep the concept in mind. Scribble down or tap in the informative pieces as you encounter them, then pull them out of the file, and practice paying back as time permits.

✳ **What to Give?** Information is probably the easiest favor to pass along. It announces that you have been thinking of that person and marks you as a source he or she can count on. It also is dispensed quickly and affords you another contact with this valuable person. Non-business information should be given only occasionally, when you're familiar with the recipient's fondest hobby, and if you are relatively close.

Whatever your choice, make it fast and simple. If it's not a tidbit of helpful news, perhaps you hold some individual in your contacts database that a cohort might profit from meeting. Nationally prominent business speaker Teena Cahill has cultivated the habit of suggesting a beneficial contact to many of the people she meets. It entices you to always open up her latest e-mail.

Remember, you seek more than mere altruism here. You are striving to establish yourself as an individual worth knowing. Sending a bottle of wine to a business acquaintance on her birthday is a thoughtful gesture and notes you as a nice guy. But it fails to establish you as a worthwhile resource.

ATTITUDE ADJUSTMENT. Cultivate judicious generosity. As daily distractions assault, it's difficult to raise our vision above our own needs and gaze on an expanded business picture. But the benefits are manifold. Try to think, like the thoughtful lass standing before the thrift shop clothing rack, "Well, this won't fit me, but I bet it would fit my friend handsomely." You will not only win gratitude, but a greater awareness.

BLUNDERS TO AVOID. Don't fawn. Offer your favors as an unattached gift between equals. The slightest whiff of obsequiousness announces loudly (and wrongly) that you are trying to insinuate your way into this person's good graces.

Also, don't get too hung up on one or two individuals. Cast your bread widely upon these waters and contact many folks. Don't call anyone too frequently.

TIPS & TASKS. Such scale balancing may be done by e-mail or with a quick phone call. The sheer surprise of this personalized piece of information makes your e-mail appreciated, and opened. Phoning it in is more effective and allows for further conversation. Try both. Keep a file on your hand held device or a special pad and note down certain interesting people or bits of information so you can send them out later. **BB**

Unleashing the Spirit

Dr. Stephen G. Payne – CEO, Leadership Strategies, Inc.

"Not one of my executives seems to be able to make a decision," complains the company owner.

"How much of that situation are you willing to own, Mr. CEO?" responds Stephen G. Payne, founder of Leadership Strategies. After some questioning, Payne's CEO admitted that he often withheld information and kept his staff terrified. Without thinking, he would cut people off or make snide remarks when their opinions differed.

Slowly, accepting his responsibility for his employees' actions, our CEO rose gratefully and pumped Payne's hand. He thanked him and promised to check himself in the future. He would share information, and stop the denigrating remarks. "No you won't," replied Payne. "Not if you are counting on raw will power alone. You've got to dig deeper."

✴ **Lead Yourself First.** Sheer clenching discipline will not banish our CEO's destructive flaws – or yours. By digging deeper, Payne was proposing the leader launch a journey of discovery – leading himself through his own mind and spirit to unearth the reasons motivating his actions. Was withholding information a way of keeping control? Were the snide remarks a way of asserting power? Such a delicate teasing apart of soul, mind, and experience is no simple achievement in any environs. Conducting such an uneasy examination within the war zone of your tumultuous business day is daunting indeed.

Those able to attain this self-understanding will find that leadership is less a matter of discipline or inherited qualities and more a path of following one's own unhindered drives.

✳ **On to Understanding Others.** The leader's journey of self-discovery never ends, but along the way he will gradually begin to observe the motivations of others, as well. To help with this understanding, Payne offers a few premises:

1. Every individual holds within himself a creative urge for good. Call it his spirituality, call it what you will, this innate force is demonstrated in that passion to build and create beneficial things. From cathedrals and song lyrics to that exactingly proportioned back stoop, each of us humans embraces that force and wants to be out there creating.

2. It becomes the manager's job to discover how that force best expresses itself in each team member, then work to unleash it in the workplace. In short, find what these individuals require, give them the tools, and stand back. (Hint: if supervisors in your organization are frequently heard to be saying to more than one employee, "Well, just lock up when you are done," this spiritual force is probably being unleashed.)

3. The final realization comes to the leader when he sees that maybe, just maybe, that spiritual force inside each individual is actually just a part of one greater force motivating far more than my workplace. But that is stepping into an advanced journey... .

ATTITUDE ADJUSTMENT. Learn to operate on the precept that you hold a certain responsibility for others' actions. Don't inflate it. Not every person's every move is responding to your grand personal power. Merely see the interactive potential. Begin an honest spiritual journey through your psyche and seek out your motivations. Firmly, lead yourself first – then others.

Believe in people's ability to astound you. It is amazing how plants can blossom given the right soil.

BLUNDERS TO AVOID. Don't give yourself excuses. Get rid of the idea that any traits are built-in, unchangeable elements of your character that you (and others) will just have to endure.

Beware of motivating team members to perform only tightly defined job tasks. Pushing unwilling souls into prescribed duties is a difficult, usually futile con job. Personal fulfillment, not filling job slots, is where the greatest performance lies.

TIPS & TASKS. What drives the people around you? Do you hold any power to unleash their spirits, even if you are not officially their manager/leader? **BB**

Managing Meetings

The Reverend Nurhad Tomeh – Presbyterian Church Synod of Lebanon/Syria

Meetings are where decisions get made. Secondarily, they may also provide avenues for catching insight into coworkers, sharing updates on groups' projects and gossip, lassoing yourself into the loop, and raising everyone's opinion of your inestimable capabilities.

But when everyone pushes away from the table bearing stale doughnuts and coffee, business plans will be laid. Whether you participate in them or not, these plans affect your company and you. So what can you do to make your voice the one most influential at these gatherings?

❋ **Passionate Objectivity.** Rev. Nurhad Tomeh sits before groups of Iraqi Christians who have just had their churches bombed, with many seeking a most unchristian strategy of preemptive armament. Another day, he sits as liaison among a group of Muslim, Jewish, and Christian women in Lebanon, each injured for religious reasons by the other side, yet all gathered for the goal of incipient peace.

His meetings make your office turmoil look like a school picnic. Much of a person's influence, Tomeh feels, comes from his or her projected image. "People accept the words of the individual whom they perceive as trustworthy, on their side, sincere, and wise," he says. Such perceptions may be formed from long experience with the group or by a brief assessment during that meeting alone. To create his own influential image, Tomeh is an ardent listener and strives to be totally honest. "It not only clears extraneous tangents and gets straight to the issue. It makes you perceived as a trustworthy character," he says.

Part of Tomeh's honesty is displayed as a measured objectivity. In most all cases he quietly states his case without bias. Then, on those few, select issues that he really seeks to drive his point across, he unleashes a measured amount of passion. The listeners take note at this atypical change and are more likely persuaded.

❋ **Pounce on the Moment.** With every issue that runs round the meeting table, there comes a golden moment. The group is getting bored with this problem; they've heard all the discussion they want to hear. Everybody wants to move on. At that point, the very next solid idea will be the one that's adopted. Study your group, see when this golden moment occurs, and then wade in modestly with that gem of a solution you've been holding back.

❋ **Script a Bit.** Few of us speak well in front of others. Fewer still are those who can convincingly respond off the cuff when a topic drops out of nowhere. One professor I know, whose trade inevitably subjects him to academia's countless and dreary meetings, always comes armed with a single sheet on which he has concisely written out his position on certain agenda points. It takes only a few moments beforehand, but his cogent words are invariably attended like a breath of pure air.

Finally, remember your goals. You are sitting around this table to enhance the meeting agenda and enhance your own position. Let your words, body language, and actions promote that agenda. Your position will rise as others acknowledge your contributions.

ATTITUDE ADJUSTMENT. Practice enthusiasm. Interminable, soporific, futile, time wasting – walk through the meeting room door with any of these preconceptions and your chances for self-enhancement are doomed. Doubtless, many meetings agonizingly fit all these adjectives. But like it or not, here you sit. Radiate boredom and your stock will plummet in your peers' eyes. Get actively involved, pitch in with solutions to your best ability, and you will make a real mark.

If the meeting topics are truly loathsome, try sparking your interest by practicing your negotiating and persuasive skills. (Gently, thank you.)

BLUNDERS TO AVOID. Seek to be the last voice, not the first. Even though you may instantly have the final solution to the proposed problem, hold off a bit, listen to others. You may be able to piggyback your idea on someone else's and gain further support.

Don't say what you feel. Avoid using the term, "I always feel...". You are meeting to find solutions. Present yours as "something that might work." Let it come from your brain, not your gut. Others will connect the plan with you and give you credit.

TIPS & TASKS. At your next meeting, mentally go around the room and make a list of each individual's motivations and needs. What inspires their decisions? Knowing these will help you understand the group's dynamic and how to better proceed toward goals.

The two times to talk at a meeting are when you have something solid to add and when you are complimenting someone else for a good idea. Other verbiage simply dilutes the effectiveness of your influence. **BB**

The Jargon Faucet

Bob Baker – CEO, Technical Copy to Go

" 'OurREAD' is a next-generation platform for delivering healthcare imaging Software as a Service (SaaS), which capitalizes on the market disturbance resulting from the convergence of Internet technologies with advanced medical data transmission and storage. The platform reverses the traditional paradigms and releases care delivery organizations..."

And this means?

Bob Baker looks at this mess of verbiage and translates it into Human. For example, "Jersey City, NJ, May 16, 2012 – An ultrasound reveals a suspicious growth on a pregnant woman's fetus. Panic! Then instant relief as a team of top obstetricians from around the world examines the image and declares it normal.

"Science fiction? No, a scientific breakthrough made possible by OurREAD, Inc.... leading the next revolution in transmission of high-definition medical images via the Internet."

A little clearer now? Baker, CEO of Technical Copy To Go, has made a fine career of translating jargon and fuzzy concepts into understandable English. His clients pay big money for this ability, and his readers adore him.

The primary intent of opening your mouth to speak or swarming your fingers over that keyboard should be to communicate some worthy idea to an audience. To make this work, your message must be in a form they understand. Makes sense. But there are a host of secondary reasons why we speak or write, and these reasons frequently obscure this primary intent.

All of us want to put ourselves in the best light, and so we often speak to impress, as well as inform. Now, a little euphemism never really

62

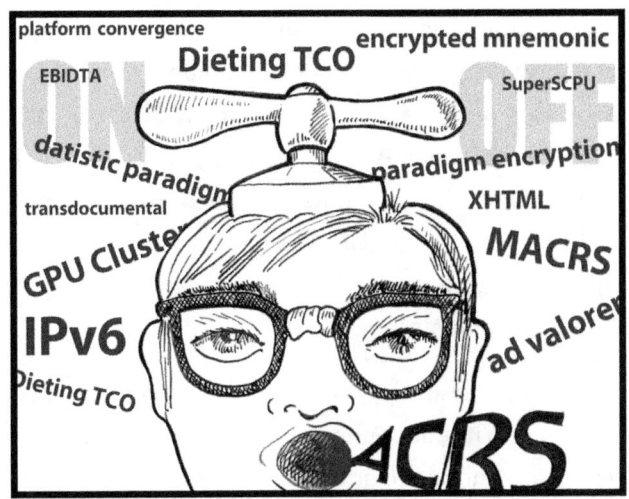

"Jargon is a characteristic language of a particular group, such as thieves." – Ambrose Bierce

hurts. To say that "I've taken some serious hits in the market," when your pushcart just got smashed by a truck is fine for class reunion chatter. But when you strut forth words and terms to display an exclusive knowledge, watch out. While these terms may announce to listeners that you dwell in that rarefied fraternity of the knowledgeable, they also obscure your meaning to the uninitiated. Such jargon cuts you and your ideas out of their sphere of interest. Better to let folks infer your brilliance from the quality of your ideas.

✳ **One Man's Jargon.** We are not suggesting you avoid technical terms entirely. Jargon, in its best usage, is an invaluable tool. It abbreviates and saves mountains of excessive explanation. One three-word Latin phrase shared between attorneys can codify paragraphs of situation, ramifications, and precedent. It's quick and handy. The question is, with whom are you sharing it?

Defined by Ambrose Bierce's *The Devil's Dictionary*, "jargon is a characteristic language of a particular group, such as thieves." Admittedly a harsh example, but it brings home the point that when you step outside your coterie, it's time to adjust your speech accordingly. Know when to turn the jargon faucet off and on.

I have one banking friend who employs his own jargon to so total an extent that I must phone for an explanation following his every e-mail. Now, I am fairly conversant with many financial and investing terms, but when they are streamed in with science fiction references and allusions to family members and individuals at meetings I've not attended, I get boggled. He is so busy working out his thoughts in each missive that his reader is not considered and gets left completely out of the picture.

Frequently, it is impossible to avoid all rare and complex terminology in explanations. Without condescension, try to follow the term with a brief definition and move quickly on. Baker always suggests emphasizing a complex technique or product by employing physical, meaningful examples, e.g., We've developed a toxin that, in a four-pint dose, would foul all of Lake Erie.

✳ **Metaphor vs. Analogy.** Enlivening your speech/writing with literary allusions certainly makes your ideas more poignant, fun, and easier on your audience. Yet unless you and your listeners always share the same books, it's best to stick to analogies, rather than metaphors. If you say "this software sets you as free to roam as Huck Finn on his raft," even if they've never heard of Mark Twain's great novel, listeners can still encompass the concept. But if you remark that "that is a very Gordian question," those unfamiliar with the Greek myth of the Gordian knot will, like Huck, be up the river.

Finally, if you want to avoid paying Bob Baker big bucks, strive to keep both sentences and words short. Some authors seem to have suckled since birth a venomous phobia to the single syllable word. Such writers never "use" words, they "utilize" them. Yet syllables seldom add clarity, and often enough they detract from real verbal punch. If you doubt the power of short words and phrases, read Ernest Hemingway.

ATTITUDE ADJUSTMENT. Concentrate first on your listeners and delivering your message to them in the most appealing way. Hold onto your pride of intellect. You are, after all, a bright soul. But don't cheat and go for complexity of vocabulary. That's too transparently easy. Rather, display your star by presenting a crisp, cogent idea whose explanation you have wittily refined. Better than complex, people will begin to see you as profound.

TIPS & TASKS. Whatever your project, company, or job, keep filling your quiver with fun, inventive ways to describe it. Memorize them and have them ready for various audiences. **BB**

Listening Is Asking

Eileen Sinett – CEO, Comprehensive Communication Services

They sat in a circle. Business leaders ranging from a medical manufacturer to a consultant on laughter. They had gathered to hear presentation coach Eileen Sinett, in one of her *Speaking That Connects* seminars. To each in turn Sinett queried, "What is listening?"

One by one, they doled out various methods of restraining one's own eager mouth and perking up one's senses to the speaker. All partially correct things to do – but each a negative, passive approach.

Only "Jill" suggested a positive course: "Listening is asking – giving those encouraging verbal signals that urge the speaker to bring out his full story."

* **Sparking the Story.** Most speakers, good or bad, constantly check their audience for clues of approval. Listeners may register this approval with a simple upturned "Um-hum" and a nod, but that goes only so far. To really help the speaker craft his tale takes your involvement. Instead of leaving him to hang in anxious monologue, you may get more of what you want to hear by providing a series of feeder questions.

The trick with these questions is to shape them so that they may be quickly inserted as one-line encouragers, rather than interruptions or invitations to a tangent. Suppose some newly met person at a conference is explaining his business, his product, and whom it serves. Examine these feeder questions asked by the listener to approve and urge on his conversation:

"I take it they are the majority of your longer-term clients, right?"

"That must be pretty difficult to niche in that tight a field, isn't it?"

"Is it tough to keep accurate controls (assessment, feedback) on that kind of process?"

With each of these questions, the asker is giving the speaker a choice. The speaker can quickly go on with just a "Yes, that's right," or he can embellish his story with a more involved answer. You are still giving him control, so you are not interrupting. If you fear these questions might lead the speaker away from his intriguing story, simply state them as comments. Instead of ending with "right?" or "isn't it?", start the line with "I'll bet..." or "It must be..."

✳ **Directing the Flow.** "All right already. This guy has a fascinating job and a very interesting business. But he's not telling me what I want to know." Now it's time for you, as listener, to custom tailor this speaker's story to what you desire to learn. It's a subtle process, demanding a bit of considered delicacy.

To slightly shift the conversation toward what the listener wants, he may simply take the gloves off his basic feeder questions. Instead of phrasing them so they may be answered by a simple yes or no, ask for more complete answers, e.g.,

"Well, then, who makes up your client base for that?"

"It's a sweet niche there, but what kind competition do you have hemming your sides?"

"Tell me a bit about how you maintain good control data on that process?"

The key here is timing and perhaps a little patience. Bring in your redirectional inquiries when the talk presents a natural segue. Don't hit the speaker with a barrage of marketing questions when he's only given you one sentence defining his product. Wait until he gets around to the topic of selling or the type of customers he's attracting.

✳ **Moving On.** Every conversation has a natural ending. This signal, alas, is not always recognized by the speaker. At most business gatherings, people want to strike, make a connection, and move on and continue flushing out other game. There's not always a graceful way to make an exit. There's a real limit to the number of times you can feign a vibrating cell phone call in your pants pocket. Whatever your choice of exits, be prepared to wrap up the conversation with a compliment and a specific invitation for further connection, (assuming you want one).

"Gee Rebecca, you've really impressed me with..."

"Good for you Joan, I admire the way your firm..."

No need to be sappy. Merely make reference to one of the speaker's strong points and let her know you'd like to hear more about it further.

ATTITUDE ADJUSTMENT. Look for the value in each presentation. Concentrate on some nugget – anything you might hear that might serve or interest you. A speaker is not someone who is taking up time until you get your chance to talk. He is offering a learning opportunity. See it as such. Get hungry for the knowledge you want and employ active listening to get yourself fed. You'll bring home a lot more – including the good opinion of those around you.

Also, adjust your attitude to the speaker and topic. Sometimes it pays for listeners to try the "gawk, tousle, shucks" approach, standing a bit wide-eyed, allowing the speaker to impress them with his expertise. Other occasions, the listener may learn more by acting as a conspiratorial fellow expert. ("As you and I both know... .") Slipping in a few pieces of appropriate jargon or statistics signals the speaker he is chatting with one of his own. He may nix the standard explanations intended for the laity and cut, thankfully, to the chase.

BLUNDERS TO AVOID. Instead of mentally scripting your own rebuttal or reply, concentrate on the speaker's words. If some particularly witty bon mot strikes you, just tuck it away for later and get back to focusing your full and total attention on the speaker.

Beware of personal money questions. Generally, don't even ask a business person about money until he brings up the topic. Best to ask about the financial potential of the whole field or market niche, rather than prying into his individual markup or net profit. "Can you really make any money at that?" is a query best left to old friends and venturists. Don't interrogate. As a journalist, it took me a long time to overcome the habit of firing one question after another. Let the speaker bring out his story in his own good time.

TIPS & TASKS. Without telling them, practice listening to the story of some forgiving friend. Work to bring out his or her tale, then try to redirect it toward some tangential topic. Later, try it on a stranger of no business importance to you. While you are listening, memorize three separate pieces of the speaker's body language that reveal insight into her character. ▆

The Employee Contract – Employers' Side

Paul Dorf – Founder, Compensation Resources, Inc.

From time to time, an unspoken contract needs to be announced out loud, just to make sure we all still get it. Ever since humans first traded goods for services, there has been the understanding that the employee would be given a workable, favorable environment in which to perform his labor. The Bible records that Hebrew masons revolted when their Egyptian bosses expected them to meet their daily brick quota without the necessary straw. Three thousand years later, most employers see the light.

We don't expect our bookkeeper to adeptly balance the accounts in a rat-swarming office with leaky steam pipes. Nor do we expect our head of marketing to create great campaigns when her supervisor is threatening to couple sexual performance with job performance. And just to make sure we take this contract to heart, the government has passed little prods of legislation. OSHA, designed to keep workplaces healthy, and various harassment laws aimed at promoting a psychologically unfettered performance, are to be flouted at the employer's peril.

But Paul Dorf, founder of Compensation Resources, Inc., says this negative, minimally-conducive-environment approach is far from effective enough in motivating company members. A 38-year veteran at guiding companies toward innovative compensation strategies, Dorf says, "I once mentioned that our company's best asset goes home every night and if we don't treat them right, they won't come back. Now I would further expand that to say we must do a whole lot more than just having them return. In a larger scope, how well an individual is treated directly affects the production of that individual."

Dorf, a master at using of all kinds of compensation, states that an employer's best investment is spent making employees feel comfortable physically, emotionally, mentally, even spiritually. He cites Abraham

Maslow's time honored Hierarchy of Needs (see below), noting that each person innately strives to be the best of what he or she can be. The wise employer realizes that he owes it both to his workers, and his shareholders to:

— make people feel secure in their job. (They have to believe their position will be there tomorrow.)

— give workers a sense of belonging within the company.

— induce confidence by providing respect for them and their efforts.

— give them a sense of achievement, within an atmosphere that unleashes their capabilities.

So forget legal compliance, and forget meeting just enough of the contract to have employees keep showing up. Invest your executive time and company money into the full range of individual needs. Then stand back and watch the magic.

ATTITUDE ADJUSTMENT. Value each employee and the staff as a whole. Wake up to the reality that your company's prime asset is its people. This is true even in the sole proprietorship. It's not your time-tested, fabulously selling widgets that keep you in business, not the brand name, not even just the sales force. Your firm thrives only when every soul in the shop stands ready to improve your product, or create a new one, and use their utmost inspiration to market it. Realizing this concept is a first step. Secondly, you will have to train your mind's eye to be aware of individual and group employee needs that will ever boost motivation. Don't be afraid to ask or experiment.

BLUNDERS TO AVOID. No amount of whippings or salary increases can make bricks without straw. Be sure you are asking the possible.

If you consider yourself "above" the team, your team will catch on soon enough and respond accordingly. Dorf tells of one client whose heart-rending speech fairly well convinced his employees of the need for salary cuts – until he drove to work in his new Rolls Royce.

Don't keep secrets. Don't hold secret executive sessions. Instead, maintain an overall sense of belonging. Let praise and calls for sacrifice be shared. Broadcasting good news, bad news, even small notes of progress solidifies the staff's feeling of being a cohesive team.

TIPS & TASKS. Realistically, no employer can meet every individual's fantasy work conditions. Employees will always labor under at least one leaky pipe. What you cannot supply, you should at least acknowledge. Saying, "I know it's tough, Marion, to produce that kind of quality under so short a deadline. Wish we could give you the time you really need. But thanks for doing your best," goes a long toward making Marion feel that needed appreciation. **BB**

The Employee Contract – Employees' Side

Joseph Petrovics – Sculptor, Ground Zero Monument

Perhaps even less discussed is the worker's side of the tacit employee contract. While the employer agrees to provide a favorable environment, the employee agrees to three things:

- To make the best of that environment as it is.

- To perform the work as best he can, without interfering with others.

- And to improve his work nest, if possible, so he may comfortably increase production and satisfaction.

"As it is" means being reasonable. The diva who stomps off the stage screaming, "I cannot work under these conditions," becomes a workplace joke and ripe for early replacement. Likewise, don't try telling your boss that you couldn't finish that report because your company-provided laptop did not have a type face you liked.

✳ **Improve Your Tools.** Joseph Petrovics' studio doesn't look a thing like your workshop. It doesn't even look like any other world-class sculptor's workshop. Casting your eyes down his tool bench, you can easily identify this as a hammer and that as some sort of chisel, but the handles seem all gnarly and misshapen.

Petrovics, following a tradition of his cobbler father back in Hungary, custom designs all his own tools to fit his hand and the task. Upon receiving the commission for the World Trade Center's 56' x 6' bronze mural commemorating the fallen firefighters of 9/11, he first sculpted tools to fit the enormous endeavor of creating that monument.

No law says that a hammer must be a straight, milled dowel proceeding at right angles from the head. Maybe the traditional format for that report, that event, or that sales procedure requires some adapting to best suit your individual talents. Innovative adjustment probably would bring you greater satisfaction. You owe it to yourself and to the company you've signed on with to keep alert and view each operation with an eye toward improvement.

Also, assess your personal space. Most work areas are set up for right-handed people. Your workflow may change from project to project. Step back, envision, and rearrange. As avid bicycle riders say, if your butt gets tired before your legs do, it's time for a change.

ATTITUDE ADJUSTMENT. First, accept reality. Even Google cannot offer its employees heaven full feasted. When you shipped with your current employer, you knew what conditions were like on board. Hopefully, you chatted unofficially with other employees, toured the premises, and scoped out the company from several angles online. If not, shame on you. Do it now.

Utterly loathsome coworkers, unbelievable deadlines, and daily distractions are part of everyone's work day – not just yours. Honest, you can adapt and struggle forward, just as all of your fellow coworkers are doing.

Secondly, be flexible to change. More easily said than done, of course. But the more you genuinely try to incorporate mandates from above into your workflow and consider suggestions from coworkers, the better your odds of finding improvement.

BLUNDERS TO AVOID. Don't be the office volcano – ready to unsettle the team at every inconvenience. Even if you are right, being the first with three disgruntled gripes in a row will brand you as a complainer to be shunned. Conversely, don't cower. When some aspect of the job environment hinders progress, bring it up with the attitude of an individual who sincerely seeks to better the productivity of the team.

 TIPS & TASKS. Review your work station and tools. What "hammer" can you reshape for greater efficiency and comfort? **BB**

Remember the Telephone?

Surinder Sangh – Owner, Crown of India Restaurant

A few months ago, I received a personal telephone call from Surinder Sangh, owner of the Crown of India Restaurant about five miles from my home. Now, my wife and I are scarcely what you would term live-wire patrons. We drop by, probably monthly, always greet Surinder as he warmly shakes our hands, and we push away from his table marvelously well fed – usually just the two of us.

Mr. Sangh had never phoned my home before, but this time he wanted to make sure that we were aware of his restaurant's upcoming Diwali celebration. Diwali means several things to India's Hindu, Sikh, and Buddhist believers. It is the festival of lights, the triumph of good over evil in the new year, the homecoming of legendary King Rama, and more. But one vital ingredient in every Diwali celebration is feasting. Mountains of absolutely superb morsels are laid out in an endless array of tempting dishes.

Beyond making your mouth water, my point is that restaurateur Sangh took the time to phone me personally. He could have e-mailed me (where it most likely would have landed in my junk file and gotten deleted.) He could have mailed a flyer (like I do not get enough junk mail already?) He could have texted me. (In turn, I could have skimmed the first three words of it on my tiny screen and probably not scrolled down.) You get the idea. For this situation, a phone call from the owner supplied the perfect marketing tactic. And by the way, it worked. We went and loved it.

When to Phone. For certain occasions, the phone still rings just the right note. Some of these include:

✳ New service demonstrations. Invite first, second, or even third tier clients. Divide the list among the senior staff and compare the responses with those obtained by other communication methods.

✹ New product calls. The company owner or even the product's creator can phone to announce a product's launch, and provide the feeling that this individual is on the short, select list. Keep the tone informal, but be sure to include your position as company head in the introductory sentences. Make it distinct from the regular phone pitch from the usual salesperson, who can come to demonstrate the new product later, if desired.

✹ Settling an argument or sticky encounter. Five minutes of personal chatting on the phone can dig you out of a hole created by scores of impersonal e-mails and texts.

✹ To distill any written report over 500 words. Summarize it verbally, then announce that the longer, written version is on its way for more complete study. (Betters your odds of getting the text read.)

✹ First-time invitations to lunch or special meetings. (At least you'll arrive knowing each other's voice.)

✹ Some thank you's. Normally people prefer a physical note they can hang on to. But sometimes promptness is more important.

✹ Seeking substantial information. If you want more than a paragraph of material, first request it by phone. Then, during the conversation, decide mutually the best way to transfer the information you need.

✹ Before shipping or after receiving any complex material. Calling, rather than a quick e-mail, indicates that you value both the package and its recipient.

✹ Requesting any favor.

✹ When you absolutely, positively must make sure the message has landed.

ATTITUDE ADJUSTMENT. Be aware of each message's optimum medium. The telephone is no longer business's swift winged Mercury. Electronic texts the size of an encyclopedia can vibrate your thigh instantaneously from callers across the globe. So save the laptop and hand-held device for the fast and furious. Let the telephone settle back into the more personal and more relaxed mode. The people whose numbers you actually "dial" now are those select few. Make them feel as if they are on the short list.

BLUNDERS TO AVOID. When addressing anyone face to face, GET THE DARN PHONE OUT OF YOUR EAR. YOU LOOK STUPID AND DISCOURTEOUS. Don't make important phone calls in restaurants or other places filled with background noise.

Also, know when to ring off. Being personal and chatty may be fine, but business people have places to go. If the conversation will demand more than a minute, ask at the outset if this is a good time. Being abrupt is bad, but droning on endlessly is an absolute sin. Brevity is the soul of sales and the "guy who can't shut up" goes hungry.

TIPS & TASKS. Pre-plan your call like a well written memo. Before punching the number, list the points you want to cover; then put them in order. Also, writing down one catchy phrase is fine, but scripting more than one sentence destroys any hope of sincerity. When you meet with someone, make a point of very visibly shutting off your phone and remarking that you want to avoid interruptions. **BB**

Afterthoughts

❊ As you converse, be always mindful of two things: the other person's needs and how this person may benefit you. Then talk as if only his needs were on your mind.

❊ Others' praise is your best advertisement. You can gain such acclaim only if you are exceptionally generous, your product is excessively cheap, or both of are of exceptional quality.

❊ Never go to a meeting to "network." It brands you as a user. Instead cross the threshold intent on making new friends.

❊ No one is convinced by what is best. People are convinced by what they believe serves them best.

❊ Everybody on your team is closet producer. If you want to succeed, it becomes your job, regardless of your station, to find that potential and help drag it out into the sunlight.

❊ The more one cares about rank and position, the less he focuses on achievement – his own or anyone else's.

❊ There are two kinds of a fool. One says, "This is tried and true, therefore it is good." The other says, "This is new, therefore it is better."

❊ Victories are won not by the team with the best players, but by the team whose players play best together. That's the true competitive edge.

❊ There's a lot in you that's admirable. A little uncluttered honesty in your daily communications will make it known. If it's not coming through, ask yourself, "What images am I putting in its way?"

❊ In negotiations, in fact everywhere, focus less on coming out on top, and more on coming away with what you want.

CHAPTER 4

Enlisting Aid

"Oh nothing important, Jenny.
Just pitching to a client, of course I have time to chat."

Prelude

The Business Community. You can almost feel her pulse wherever working men and women gather. Each of us operates as mutually dependent, mutually benefitting members of this oddly dynamic body. And she nourishes our growth.

Whether you labor as an employee in a massive corporation or run your sole proprietorship from your basement, your success depends on how effectively you enlist the aid of others in your business process. Such recruitment requires a continual, negotiative dance made up of basically two steps. First, you must make yourself into an individual with whom people will want to work. They must not only benefit from, but enjoy their experience with you. Step two is the art of the deal – learning how to bring folks aboard and not have them regret their decision later.

This chapter lays down a few footprints for both steps. As with all other tactics, you must understand the necessary mental and emotional adjustments, then adapt them to your personal style.

Inspiring Trust

Franklin Covey – Founder, Franklin Covey Insights
Jack Welch – Former CEO, GE Corporation

'Tis not love, nor greed. In business, it's trust that makes the world go 'round. Once employees trust that you have their best interests at heart, their efforts will flourish unlimited. Earn the trust of first time customers, and they will become long-term clients.

Franklin Covey has followed in father Stephen Covey's footsteps as a renowned management visionary and consultant. (Stephen authored *The Seven Habits of Highly Effective People*, in 1989.) With the whole panoply of business issues and crusades from which to choose, Franklin Convey has, very deliberately, focused everyone's attention on Inspiring Trust. In his new workshop series of the same name, Covey cites study after study in which employee innovation and overall success thrive in a climate of trust. The Frito-Lay Company's deliberate "trust makeover", directly translated into higher speed, lower costs, and a 300 percent climb in stock value.

It benefits your company to exude an atmosphere of trust. It benefits your sanity to be a trusted, trustworthy individual. Obvious.

✳ **Nurture, Not Nature.** What seems less apparent is Covey's assertion that gaining trust is a learnable skill, not a divine gift. The "I just don't trust that guy" feeling is most likely your own instinct picking up on that person's subtly suspicious actions. The methods for establishing trust are many, but a few of the initial training calisthenics include:

1. Develop Self-Trust. Examine, and be very clear about your own motives. Try taking aim at goals that fill your long-term happiness, rather than staunch this moment's yearning. Study the content of your own character, and realize the strength of your own capabilities. Learn to depend on powers you actually have, and you will lean less on a hollow image that arouses suspicion.

2. Build Relationship Trust. Likewise, learn the many special strengths of those around you, as well as their foibles. Realize both their potential as well as their track record. This will set reasonable expectations and boundaries.

3. Create Total Transparency. Talk straight. Clearly let people know your motivations, your expectations, and your exact plans. It is the executive's job not to merely explain something – but to make sure people completely understand it.

4. Confront Reality. Set goals by filling your sails with hope, but remaining ever anchored in reality. (Pessimistic or optimistic goals are not informed reality. They are merely spins on reality.)

Publish the goal to all involved. When expectations begin to fail, call people and explain, and renew the goal. Jack Welch, former CEO of GE, gained amazing trust of the financial community by setting lofty, reasonable quarterly targets, and explaining how he intended to reach them. Then, on those rare occasions when it looked as if GE might fall short, he would personally call reporters and explain why. It got so his unflinchingly honest word alone could lift stock prices. Trust moves even fiscal cynics.

5. Open Up Avenues. Put in place some formal communication/complaint/clarification channels through which individuals can express their views. These allow everybody to get the correct, updated news, without resorting to rumor.

ATTITUDE ADJUSTMENT. Enhance your trustworthiness by establishing your own self-worth, and a belief in the reliability of those around you. This involves weeding out suspicions (even the well founded ones.) Yield up a bit of control to faith. Placing belief in others opens you to all the rewards that flow from cohesive teamwork.

BLUNDERS TO AVOID. Don't hide bad news. Don't hold secret executive sessions. Despite best intentions, secrets only breed suspicion.

Also, you cannot hide your true motivations, so don't try. The sales person who drools greed can never schmooze a deal into place.

🔔 **TIPS & TASKS.** Start at the beginning. List the main acts and projects on which you are currently working. Now, honestly, list the several motives that move you in this work (not the ones you "should have," but the ones you actually feel.) Ask yourself if you would trust a person with such motives. ▣

Nearer to Thee, Dear Customer

Richard K. Rein – Founder, U.S. 1 Newspaper

Everyone knows that print newspapers are facing swords at their throats. As advertising dollars venture into an ever broader array of pastures, traditional sources must split a dwindling market share. Yet recently, Richard K. Rein, Editor, Publisher, and Founder of *U.S. 1 Newspaper*, officially, and noisily, celebrated his publication's very successful 25th year, thank you.

Launched as a shoestring venture from his Princeton, New Jersey home, *U.S. 1* has, under Rein's deft leadership, become one of the most powerful business resources in the Garden State. The *U.S. 1* business directories are considered "must haves" for the region, and companies go to extraordinary lengths to get profiled in the paper.

Part of *U.S. 1*'s 25th celebration included an insightful piece by its publisher listing about two dozen decisions that had led to the paper's quarter-century prosperity. One that proved generally applicable began when the founder was delivering the papers to readers from the back of his aged sedan. *U.S. 1* was a free paper, and then, as now, most of such papers were found in racks heaped outside office doors and in lobbies.

But Rein decided to go one step better. In each case, he – and all his subsequent delivery people – would walk into the individual business and place a stack of papers in the firm's own waiting area. If the office had a receptionist, Rein would stop and chat, and frequently gain fodder for future stories. Today, the weekly arrival of *U.S. 1* is seen as an event in most businesses and a chance to swap the latest info.

ATTITUDE ADJUSTMENT. View clients as people first and income streams second. Go that extra mile, take the few steps, and always pause to chat with everyone along the way. Additionally, that extra convenience of having the product hand delivered and more tempting to use wins not only sales, but friends. It's the inadvertent relationships that seem to initiate the turning points in business. The best way to keep open to such opportunities is to get closer to customers, vendors, and suppliers, both literally and metaphorically.

BLUNDERS TO AVOID. Never seem busy when meeting with a client. This is a hard one, particularly in an age that views being harried as a moral virtue. Instead of trying to establish the most-clients-contacted record, take a few moments. Shorten the encounter, but give each person your total attention. And for heaven's sake – Get that darn cell phone out of your ear.

Also, be wary of being too chummy. Be sensitive to each client's desired emotional space and respect it.

TIPS & TASKS. Like the Fuller brushmen of old, it may help to keep a private list of the client's (receptionist's) interests, children etc. Use it to refresh your mind before entering. Also, examine exactly where is the meeting point of the client and your service/product. How advantageous is that environment? If it is your choice, would a different venue improve the relationship? **BB**

Admirability Points

Warren Buffett – Industrialist, CEO, Berkshire Hathaway

Leadership is partially a learned skill. The military has taught it for centuries, now business is giving leadership techniques a shot. Yet with all the training and ploys, there is one factor that the leader absolutely must have – Admirability. It's not a technique or skill. It is a truth. Every time a leader turns to his team and stalwartly states, "Come on crew, let's go this way..." there is an unspoken finish to that sentence: "....and you will end up like me." In short, we follow people who possess some qualities we want to have.

✳ **As a Child.** As a young boy I idolized my father. I walked like him, used his phrases, and even tried my hand at his activities. Like millions of boys, I wanted to grow up to be just like my admirable dad. Actually, such youthful emulation wasn't a bad bet. Dad did things this way. They worked for him. Why shouldn't it work for me? Certainly, I was more likely to eventually possess his magic respect, strength, and wisdom if I followed his track, rather than some other.

As adults, it differs little. Financier Warren Buffett tells of how early in his career, he learned of Ben Graham's revolutionary investing techniques. Impetuously, Buffett hopped a train and several hours later was knocking on Graham's locked office door to sit at this guru's feet – on a Saturday. Buffett had seen a person who held some admirable ability and therefore was willing to follow. Likewise, the members on your workplace team will more likely follow the admirable voice among them.

✳ **What's Admirable?** A leader needs Admirability Points – those aspects of himself that others envy and want to possess. These need not be a masterful market wizardry or Gatesian tech savvy that has filled your living room with gold in sacks. It may be as simple as being seen as "the guy who has a history of giving the right suggestions."

You may have a serene confidence, a virtuosic control of facts, or an evident satisfaction with your career. Perhaps yours is the only calm voice in the room. Whatever your Admirability Points are, allow them to be inferred by the team members. (Subtly, subtly.) Establish your leadership first by suggestion, then by becoming a habitual resource.

✳ **Leaders & Managers Sidebar.** 'Tis a quick and popular quip to propound that American business is over managed and under led. Within the past decade the buzzword "Leadership" has drenched every consultant's report, telling how we need more of this so necessary, but elusive quality.

By a manager, we mean an individual who can make things work – fix problems and apply solutions. Leaders, we define as those who can get other people to willingly follow and help complete some task. Assessing the two, President Richard M. Nixon perceptively noted that for any major enterprise, you need managers, leaders, and people who can do both.

ATTITUDE ADJUSTMENT. Realize that you and your image are a billboard for your leadership. Gaining the necessary admirability may partially involve image building and presentation skills. But mostly, it grows from connecting with your team and letting them see what you have.

BLUNDERS TO AVOID. Please, avoid leader-like posturing. It's painfully transparent and self-destructive. You've got enough admirability points to lead at least sometimes. Concentrate on them.

Further, don't disparage managers. It is currently popular, á la Stephen Covey, to view managers as the mindless ones who are good at grubbing up the ladder, while the visionary leader makes sure the ladder's leaning against the right wall. The success of your enterprise will demand both qualities from each staff member – and you.

TIPS & TASKS. List your personal strengths that others might envy. Now, (more painfully) make an honest list of those qualities and behaviors which squelch your own leadership control. How have you seen members of your team respond to each? **BB**

Join the Throng

Not only is it your most valued resource, your time is often your greatest business bottleneck. We all see the need to invest it frugally, and time spent hob nobbing in a professional association often seems profligate.

But amidst the genial palaver and rubber chicken of the typical monthly association meeting, a great many gleaming opportunities may lie hidden. It is definitely worth browsing the trade organizations list and attending a few meetings of those related to your field. It doesn't have to be an exact fit. Many marketers have joined the National Speakers Association simply to better their presentation skills. Look to see what serves you.

* **Leadership Presence.** Particularly for the newcomer, offering your services as chapter secretary, program director, or some other seldom-sought post automatically sets your elbows rubbing with the top players in your profession. Further, it raises your and/or your firm's stature in the eyes of both members and potential clients. You may know that being organization corresponding secretary merely marks you as the recipient of long hours of thankless paperwork, but to others it shows a commitment to your profession. Like a trademark, it indicates a past and intended long future in the business.

As to which organizational post best enhances your career, watch the signs. Find out which committees attract the people you most need to know. Ask around. Then simply tell the chair or executive director that you are enamored with the organization and the XYZ committee's work and "I'd be glad to help sometime in any way." After they recover from the shock of your unsolicited offer, they'll probably usher you into your advantageous slot. Just make sure your time and skills are up to the task. You don't want to drop the ball in front of your peers.

✳ **Talking the Talk.** Like flowing fountains, professional groups gush an ever renewed supply of information and contacts. To glean the best of both requires a little planning. Before attending any meeting, sketch out your greeting elevator pitch. Have at least two or three versions at the ready which in two sentences tell what you and your company do in an optimal way. Err on the side of subtle modesty here. Remember, you are among strangers, most of whom know generally what your trade entails. And for heaven's sake, keep bringing a fresh supply of pitches. Nothing wears like a thrice-heard, stale recital.

Check out the organization's website, learn about the group's history. Find out a few facts about some of the officers that you can use when you are introduced to them. If the website has pictures, notice how the members dress for events. Yes, it's just like a job interview: these people know clients and you want to be referred.

Once at the meeting, don't be afraid to voice some of the challenges that have stumped you. If anyone holds a solution, it's your fellow professionals. You may want to hold back on touting your client list, however. After all, many of the folks in the room are competitors.

ATTITUDE ADJUSTMENT. Try to push the madding-crowd concept away from your mind and see the organizational meeting more as a fertile hunting ground for individuals of value. Joining groups may not be your thing. Many people feel claustrophobic in large gatherings. Others automatically over-ignite and need to actively rein in their explosions of ebullience. Abandon insecurities and let natural conversation flow.

BLUNDERS TO AVOID. Be careful not to overcommit. Organizations are devourers of time. If you don't watch out, they will feed you a slim diet of praise and gobble up untold hours.

Beware of politics. When you see an organizational petty turf war brewing, run, do not walk to the nearest neutral corner. There is no profit in getting embroiled in power struggles. This organization is not your career, it is only a tool to bolster it.

 TIPS & TASKS. Scour the internet; ask others in your company and within the profession what groups they have joined. Develop a list of all the professional organizations and related foundations that apply. Then find out which has the members and offerings that may best serve you and your company. **BB**

Social Media: More Intimate – Less Personal

Deborah Smith – Founder, Social Media Consulting

Technology is a wellspring of inadvertent irony. As we gleefully or grudgingly have lurched into this latest mode of pop communication, speculations run rampant as to how it has effected our basic humanity. Blogs and social media: do they separate or bind us as individuals?

The ironic answer is Yes. It always is with any newly adopted piece of technology. As several *Wired Magazine* editors have wisely noted, you do not make friends on social media. When your stalled auto leaves you stranded at 2 a.m., you do not text a Facebook contact and roust him out of the sack to come get you. You call a real friend. On the other hand, the very remoteness of cyber-companionship affords a kind of closeness that your real pal who's meeting you on the highway would never dare attempt.

Your Twitter or Facebook buddy has few compunctions about telling you to get off your high horse and quit ranting. Your LinkedIn associate feels total freedom to warn you when you are blundering toward unprofitability. In short, what we have sacrificed in personal, physical familiarity, we have, perhaps, made up for with a bit more unfettered, intimate honesty. If – big "if" – we employ blogs and social media with a dose of diligent care.

Social media consultant and serial blog entrepreneur Deborah Smith has been enlightening bewildered business people since blogs were in their infancy. "There is so much offered by social media," she says, "but as with any business venture, your benefit relates directly to how much you have studied the possibilities." For the professional seeking to gain more from social media than virtual chin-wagging and looking up old classmates, Ms. Smith and others offer a few tips.

* **Golden "To SM or not SM" Rule:** Do not deny any technological tool until you have learned to master it. Using your favorite means, learn about Social Media (SM). Do not relegate the process entirely to a coworker.

* **Know What You Want.** Say out loud what you really expect individual sites, chats, blogs, and discussion groups you're considering joining. Does this list sensibly fit with your career plans? Can this blog, etc. realistically deliver this?

* **Business vs. Social.** Whether you are establishing a personal or a corporate presence on any SM application, once you enter as a person of business, you are key-tapping in a whole new arena. As we've noted, business is a stage of constant judgment, and under the immense public interactivity of social media, the lights of scrutiny shine terrifyingly bright.

Social Media puts your entire professional reputation on the line – literally. Neglect your Facebook wall for a few months or let the Tweets pile up unnoticed as a private citizen and who cares? Yet allow queries and comments to go unanswered as a professional, and those unheeded folks will virally spread the word of their ill-treatment at cyber-speed.

BLUNDERS TO AVOID. Beware the SM time-gobbling machine. As mentioned, once into SM, your reputation chains you to it. Be sure you can commit the time. Further, contributions may be made with such ease and seeming anonymity that blogging and SM posting may become woefully addictive and hazardous to your business health. Limit your daily/weekly involvement in SM to a sensible number of minutes. Avoid trying to daily pack in X number of postings.

This can mire you into more devotion than you had planned. And always, keep monitoring the cost/benefits ratio of your involvement.

Also, remember that the "P" in Post stands for perpetual – 'til hell freezes over. And the "T" stands for "to totally everyone." So post VERY cautiously. Your "just between us" photo may be oogled over by a Mongolian yak herder today – and his grandchildren a century from now. It also may be searched out by employers, office enemies, clients, and competitors. Rule of thumb: sex, drugs, booze, and politically partisan issues draw disapproval from great segments of our society. If you don't care, fine. Simply realize the risk.

ATTITUDE ADJUSTMENT. Be aware that you are entering the realm of hardball media. There lurks the illusion that blogs and social media offer warm and cozy nooks where you may freely express your every thought to a cadre of like-minded folks. While the chatty mood and window dressing may appear like a coffee house, you are standing on the trading floor of a very aggressive exchange.

Everyone in SM is pitching to you. Even on personal sites, people seek to sell themselves – or a side of themselves – to make themselves look of interest to all those folks out there. This is not a bad thing. After all, you will learn much more about that intriguing person you met briefly at a conference – make swifter judgments – than via hours of phone and internet checking. Once aware of this, you may play the game with the best of them. So burnish up your own image and set it out for all to see. Just remember, as you have polished, so have they.

TIPS & TASKS. Try a little fishing expedition. Nearly 200 social media sites are now up and running, with blogs numbering in the untold millions. The big three – Facebook, LinkedIn, and Twitter offer a wide array of connective services, but hunting in a smaller forest may provide you better targets. In addition to Tweeting, try a few Plurks. Beyond your LinkedIn cohorts, you may benefit from connecting with a few Ryze entrepreneurs. Maybe TalkBizNow may prove equally as profitable and fun as Facebook. Professional SM applications offer countless opportunities to expand your potential client, employer, or mentor database. As with every marketing venture, it's a blend of not only enlarging the size and visibility of the billboard, but finding the best placement. **BB**

The Lust for Power

Richard Dreyfuss – Actor as "Glenn Holland"
Willie Walsh – CEO, British Airways

Some might argue that it was Richard Burton's portrayal of Alexander the Great or Marlon Brando as Godfather Don Corleone. Others might claim that Hollywood's greatest portrayal of raw power was displayed in the depiction of the empire-forging Ghengis Khan by the legendarily miscast John Wayne.

But for this writer, it was not until I viewed Richard Dreyfuss as the soft-spoken, muddled high school music teacher in the 1995 movie *Mr. Holland's Opus* that I witnessed the strongest, most powerful influence one human can express over others. A frustrated composer, Glenn Holland had sought, but never quite found solace in teaching the joys of classical music to thousands of students over the years. His unpublished, unperformed symphony hung as an albatross of failure around his neck. Finally, in an explosive finale that only Hollywood could concoct, pedagogue Glenn Holland receives his just and ample reward. Hundreds of his former students spontaneously flood back to his school and perform Mr. Holland's Opus for him as a surprise treat. The current Governor (a former student) has released a prisoner (another student) to join this symphonic throng. It is enough to make the very stones weep for joy.

Now the real life lesson here is not to expect a surprise celebratory appreciation-fest after a lifetime of management consulting. All those folks to whom you have sold software, soap, or annuities are almost assuredly not planning you a party. But there is a moral in these tales of power that we may apply throughout our careers.

※ **Power for Production.** For many of us, power is measured only by The Great Khan's yardstick of how many unwilling souls we can force to do our bidding. The man who makes 500 workers punch a clock is seen as more powerful and successful than the owner of only a ten-person firm. Trouble is, this negative capacity to wield sheer brawn and induce a fearful response holds limited charm. It signals merely that you are the richest, toughest, or most verbally compelling individual on the team.

Beware of leadership without humor. If coworkers are not laboring joyfully, you have no real power at all.

Glenn Holland's true opus was that he was able to grippingly imbue his people with such a passion that they came willingly – joyfully – to their labors. In the realm of business that is the only real power. An army of wage slaves cannot match the production nor dollars-and-cents profitability of a motivated, inspired crew.

All of us lust for power. We crave influence over others. But the achievement of Mr. Holland's greatest practical power is a matter of aim and method. It is deceptively easy and tempting in the corporate setting to wrangle your way into a position where others will do what you suggest. It seems the quickest path towards getting things done. You become known as a player – one who can achieve. But horses grow weary with continued flogging, and those conscripted to your will by your sheer might, move with increasingly uninspired sluggishness. Rather, the leader who moves his power lust away from his persona, and aims it toward the project, will find himself holding the reins of a juggernauting team. The methods capable of generating such power-for-the-project are several. Leaders can simply meet each team member on the level of his or her own motivation and design tasks that blend both this person's desire with company needs. Leaders may also personally radiate an explosive enthusiasm for the project. Watching your energies forging ahead is infectious. We all want to be set ablaze in some direction, so we catch the flame from one already afire. The mantle of leadership falls naturally on such a person's shoulders.

Even if she is not the owner or officially designated team leader, that energetic person who drives the project forward will find her opinion sought out, and others deferring to her suggestions. A little cautious playing on that ball-of-fire, full-of-solutions persona may help here. Developing the image of unspoken leadership can make your role more recognized, provided it never appears as if you're overstepping. ('Tis a tricky road here. Err on the side of restraint.)

For those already imbued with rank and authority the process of striving for power in its truest sense works equally. Individually help people motivate themselves toward the goal and establish yourself as someone both sympathetic and admirable. When an Icelandic volcano shut down all European airspace, British Airways CEO Willy Walsh boarded the first test plane to see if the skies were again safe to fly. He led his troops in searching for a solution.

Oh, and Alexander the Great, by the way? When he and his all-volunteer army landed in Persia, each man stood bound to him by personal loyalty. They utterly defeated the conscripted, slave host of Persian Emperor Darius – a force 10 times that of Alexander's.

ATTITUDE ADJUSTMENT. Hard as it is, channel your leadership energies and strategies away from your persona and toward motivating the team members. Make the project and individual contributions your central focus.

BLUNDERS TO AVOID. Beware of leadership without humor. If coworkers are not laboring joyfully, you have no real power at all.

TIPS & TASKS. Look at your company and current projects. Write down how you can make these endeavors of interest to those in your group. What methods would strike a chord of enthusiasm? **BB**

Employ Your Lawmakers

Hon. James C. Greenwood – President and CEO,
Biotechnical Industry Organization

Democracy is the rule of the most energetic. Energize yourself to meet and get your legislators on your side, and you will be much more effective.

"It's a whole lot easier than most folks seem to think, and frankly I'm surprised more individuals don't reach out to their legislators more often," remarks Jim Greenwood. He should know.

As former state Assemblyman and as Congressman for Pennsylvania's 8th district, and now as President and CEO of the Biotechnology Industry Organization (BIO), Greenwood has sat on both sides of the petitioning desk. He constantly encourages business people in all positions – employees and owners – to seek solutions through their legislators. Far beyond mere lawmaking, they have more facilities and contacts than you realize.

Since government and commerce first began, they have been inextricably intertwined. Today, our nation abounds with domestic and international trade councils, missions, and a fountain of funding sources. Employees turn to the Department of Labor and entrepreneurs find startup aid from the SBA. But there stand scores of lesser known agencies and programs serving every aspect of business. No one knows better whom to call, and no one can get you into the right door like your legislator. Assembly and Congress people are prime supporters whom you need to add to your personal network. They are used to and want to take individual petitions.

❋ **Making the Approach.** Greenwood suggests a little preparation beforehand.

1. Be aware that all legislators are used to being asked for things. Your petition is not an interruption, it is a major part of what they do.

2. Introduce yourself positively. Find which bills this lawmaker has sponsored and write a note telling him how much you appreciated his vote on one of them. Then phone an aide and tell him that the letter is on the way. This is your introduction, so make it upbeat. Now is not the time to bring up what you want, or curse his stance on bills you loathe.

Then, a bit after this introductory thank you has had time to sink in, make an appointment. More than one such note is effective and appreciated. Reassure the aide you "only require a few brief moments of the Senator's time." If it's more than just yourself, mention the number of people in your delegation, and offer to send the aide a list of who is joining you, and be sure to note who will act as spokesperson.

3. At the Office. Do be succinct. Don't be shy. Don't rush the romance. Before you go in, have a very clear mental script of what you want – and how you'll communicate it. The first sentence should introduce you and your business position, and immediately express appreciation for some vote or his general stance on certain issues. Then at your next opportunity to speak, get straight to what you seek in clear, distilled, and razor-precise sentences. Have the appropriate bill number and specific passages with you. Know the bill's status thus far.

Time permitting, you might bring up a few common connections, but you didn't come here today to make a friend. When this meeting is completed, write a thank you note, make sure you are on his e-mail list, and then seek ways to further the relationship.

✳ **Legislative Assessment.** In truth, there are very, very few legislators who are not very, very sharp. You should be as talented in your own field. They've been long trained at quickly taking in strange concepts and translating them into plans of action. It's their trade. As for clout, your vote and your effort to reach out provide more influence than you might think. Legislators do take note, and they tend to see petitioners as representative of a larger voting constituency. For this reason, you are worth their time. Those who seek meetings seldom cool their heels for very long.

Of course, your Assemblyperson probably will not wrench the law from its sockets just to serve you or your firm. However, lawmakers are deal makers; they have magic they can work that most likely will ameliorate the situation. Finally, yes. There exist legislators who are cash cozy with major lobbyists. But even bought-and-paid-for politicians are adept at serving two masters. Odds are slim that your petition conflicts directly with some mainstream lobby. And if it does, remember, most politicians receiving funds, funnel it into war chests to seduce your vote. So work from the angle that your petition represents a larger constituency than the lobbyist can buy.

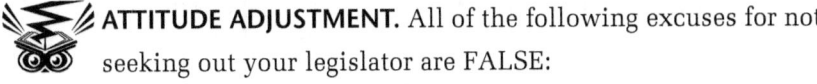 **ATTITUDE ADJUSTMENT.** All of the following excuses for not seeking out your legislator are FALSE:

"They are too dumb/ignorant to understand." says the highly technical research scientist.

"I don't have the clout," says the employee seeking betterment for his company or for himself.

"They aren't going to pass a law just to help me," says the business owner who has never visited his state or federal offices.

"I can't spend my days cooling my heels in some unapproachable Congress person's office. I have a business to run," says the executive who has never paid a call.

"They are all corrupt $#@&! who are wholly owned by the huge corporate lobbyists," says the business person whose only legislator-visions come from nightly news sound bites.

BLUNDERS TO AVOID. The 20-minute preamble on your industry's value to America since Thomas Jefferson, or a litany of your personal woes are guaranteed deal breakers. There will be time enough to explain the obstacles briefly after the lawmaker understands your petition and asks for the history. Be deadly honest and straight-forward, warns Greenwood. "You cannot shock a legislator," he says. "But the slightest whiff of a hidden motive or something misleading will banish your effectiveness."

Finally, leave your anger at home. You don't respond favorably to fire-breathing complainers storming into your office. Your congress-person won't either.

TIPS & TASKS. Other contact methods may include: going to his website and opening his e-mailing box. Also watch for her schedule in her newsletter and attend her next town hall meeting or fund raisers. Be a grass roots lobbyist and throw a large picnic fund raiser for family, firm members, and friends, and invite this legislator. (Lots of folks do this. It's fun and makes great legislator flypaper.) **BB**

A Pat on Both Your Backs

Alberto Molina – CEO, SureTech.com

Myth has it that if you are stingy with giving credit, more folks will believe that you achieved things all by yourself. Credit, they feel, is a pie, from which every slice given to you means one less for me. This, in short, is just not so.

The uniquely brilliant Isaac Newton invented differential calculus alone in his study and then claimed to have seen further than others only because he had "stood on the shoulders of giants." Those who display themselves as fearlessly generous with credit are, not surprisingly, more often admired as self-assured and a resource for talent.

✳ **Blow Their Horn.** Recently, I witnessed Alberto Molina, founder of SureTech.com, take a client through one of his most creative and complex websites. His presentation was constantly laced with "Matt suggested this feature..." and "David and Josh implemented that little... ." I didn't know these names, but I couldn't miss the pride he was placing in his team. The client came away realizing that SureTech was a multitalented force, rather than a one-man geek show depending on a sole "creative person." From Alberto's perspective, the entire sales pitch became much easier when he could openly brag about the team's achievements, rather than awkwardly endeavoring to subtly inflate his own personal feats.

✳ **A Thank of the Pen.** Crediting others' advice and ideas also reflects well on the writer of any corporate report. The supervisor who acknowledges a long list of contributing sources establishes himself as a team leader, able to galvanize others into action. It also gives the report further credibility. In all business writing, authors should seek to move away from personal opinion, into the realm of thoughtful, supported conviction.

Remember, making a personal acknowledgment to the contributing individual is just as important as a mention in the final presentation. In measuring out your praise, be selective. Don't hold back on any substantial, honest contribution. Yet too much, slathered on too frequently, ruins your credibility.

ATTITUDE ADJUSTMENT. To make your accreditation honest, you'll have to become a team player. You cannot simply say Sharon contributed a lot. You've got to invite her into the game and make her part of it. Get her emotionally invested in it. This is not always easy, and certainly is not ideal for every job. Sometimes he travels fastest who travels alone. You've got to determine if bringing in another individual would enhance the final outcome.

BLUNDERS TO AVOID. Get real. Get wary. There abound plenty of credit vultures who perch with talons poised, ready to rip away your hard work or hard won ideas and claim them as their own. Sometimes you can thwart this by branding the work in a way that makes it instantly recognizable as yours. Often, you can claim an initial copyright on the work by subtly broadcasting that you are plugging away on a project and currently are weighing several solutions. This way, the credit thief's last minute swoop-in will be seen for what it is.

TIPS & TASKS. Look at the last projects you have just completed. Who was involved that you did, or did not recognize – either to themselves, or in the final presentation? Now, examine your current task at hand. How would gaining and crediting some additional input enhance your own status? ▣

Afterthoughts

❋ The best way to enlarge your circle of beneficial acquaintances is to be both powerful and generous. The miserly powerful dine alone. Or, of course, you can simply be entertaining.

❋ Joining organizations and committees is the most frustrating, time-gobbling, and essential method of growing your business and career.

❋ When enlisting aid, be ever precise as to what you want. Are you asking for a contact when you really seek a client?

❋ Pour out your praise like a moderate priced wine. Not like a fine, rare vintage held always in reserve; nor like a gush of water that dilutes each drop's flavor.

❋ Three things sour your odds in any negotiation: a little anger, a little liquor, and a lot of pretense.

❋ Don't tally favors too strictly. Business is more a process of creating mutual benefit than balancing obligations in a scale.

❋ Before seeking anyone's service, learn her motivations. Then accordingly add a dab of subtle grease, such as a compliment or personalized tidbit of information.

❋ Would you help out a person like you? If so, you probably radiate a certain openness, trustworthiness, and a little hint that you hold some benefit in your pocket.

BB

CHAPTER 5

Selling Your Abilities

Fifty percent of the people are too shy to market themselves.
48 percent are only too eager.

Prelude

Business is built on reputation. The truth is, your work may speak for itself, but it will not necessarily speak for you. People need to be shown the link between your deeds and the individual who authors them. It is your job to show them. Making this connection is among the most subtle and most vital aspects of business success. And few of us do it well.

People feel fine touting their company or product, but when it comes to holding up our own light, most of us are either too shy or all too annoyingly eager. Being American gives you an edge. We are tolerant of self-selling. Ours is one of the few cultures in which failing to sell yourself is considered arrogant. But still, the art of letting your personal excellence gradually, yet distinctively, dawn on others requires delicate handling.

This chapter offers a few tactics for branding yourself in others' minds. More than any chapter, readers might pay special attention to the Blunders to Avoid notes. And of course, remember, the greatest self-selling blunder is neglect.

Marketing Your Primary Product

Ilise Benun – Founder, Marketing Mentor

Nobody better promotes a company than its owner. He knows every little process and cranny of the plant, every strong point of the product, and his emotional enthusiasms for his life/business calling are contagious. So it is with you, promoting yourself. Nobody can do it better.

Let's be honest. You really do think you are pretty wonderful and mightily skilled. (If not, you'd best look harder.) It only makes sense that others should gradually come to learn of your many talents. But before folks may stand in awe of your resume, product, or hireable intellect, they must first know you exist. This is the greatest untaken step, says Ilise Benun, founder of Marketing Mentor. Thus, those who squirm their way out their shyness shell and politely make the surrounding world aware of themselves gain a competitive edge.

Ms. Benun promotes herself and others the way you fantasize about being marketed. She has written and published six widely selling books on the topic of self promotion; she engineers frequent conferences; and she teams up with just the right experts. If Ilise is in the room, you know it. Not because she is pushy, not because because she sucks all the oxygen out of the hall with her blazing persona, but because invariably she will come up and warmly introduce herself to you.

She exemplifies her basic, three-part self-marketing strategy. If you adopt it, you will find a path that enriches your life, and profits your business.

* **Start Conversations.** Go out of your way to get into conversations with anyone and everyone you can – in person, on the phone, or via e-mail. Cross the street, cross the room, cross the train, to talk to someone. First, find out what they're working on and then

afterward tell them what you're working on. Or better yet, let them ask. Anything can come out of a simple conversation: ideas, alliances, connections, referrals, new business, new opportunities.

* **Keep in Touch** by picking up the phone. These days, so much interaction happens electronically that picking up the phone is almost a novelty. This means it will make you stand out. Plus you have the advantage of an actual dialogue. Dedicate a half hour each day to make a round of calls to keep in touch with those whom you have (or would like to have) a business relationship. This includes past, current, and possibly future customers, as well as vendors and colleagues. You never know where the work is going to come from.

* **Follow Up** absolutely every single lead that comes your way. This is where many people fall down. After the conference, stack up the business cards up THAT NIGHT and fire off an acknowledgment, even if it's only a "Nice to Meet You" boilerplate e-mail that you adjust with each person and situation. Every person whose card you get, everyone who expresses even the slightest interest in your work or says he knows someone who.... Get back to each one. Keep a log. Don't worry about response. Just keep planting seeds and initiating conversations.

ATTITUDE ADJUSTMENT. Realize that people really do want you to talk to them. Envision everyone on this globe as your casual, non-threatening lunch buddy. Half of humanity is shy about meeting strangers, another 48 percent is willing, but hasn't a clue what to say. For the shy, it is difficult to remember that all homo sapiens are basically lonely individuals who crave a kind word from any fellow taking interest in their doings.

Even in those rare instances when your conversation is rebuffed, what have you lost? Some self-absorbed soul, whom you have never met nor will meet again, will consider you a pest for a mere instant. You won't stick in her head, don't let her stick in yours.

BLUNDERS TO AVOID. Remember, this initial meeting is not the time to impress folks with your amazing prowess. Try not to lace your conversation with the patter of your little feats. Rather, view each meeting as a learning experience – filling your own personal encyclopedia.

TIPS & TASKS. As to initiating a conversation, it's often easy to develop some little humorous ice breaker. One of my favorites when standing before the elevator has been "I often wish that the harder you hit the button, the faster the elevator would come." Not particularly witty, but it got this writer an interview with the chief editor of "Esquire" magazine when he was starting out. **BB**

Card Sense

Tony Simmons – Simmons Business Services

Amidst all the greeting and flesh pressing at conventions and various meetings, you will undoubtedly acquire pockets bulging with business cards. Today, the card exchange has become a ritualistic acknowledgment, validating a business encounter as worthwhile.

☀ **Passing 'em 'Round.** How you slather acquaintances with your business cards is, of course, up to you. But be aware that the person who sits down at a table, announces his name and in a reflex motion deals out a card to one and all, will appear somewhat callous and demeaning. The presenting of a business card is, at best, a sign that you find this individual of enough interest to retain a communication. A little restraint will make it more valued. When passing your own card around to a definitely hot prospect, give him a reminder. Scribble the date and meeting venue on the back and perhaps a one-phrase description of any interesting thoughts you've shared.

☀ **And the Follow Through... .** When planning your response to a business card, consider giving those hot prospects a video follow-up.

It truly sets you apart. Tony Simmons (www.simmonsservice.com) is a master at this. His clients send marvelously effective greetings. Recipients open your e-mail and there you sit in your office chair saying, "Hello Carol, I really enjoyed talking with you at the software seminar yesterday... ." Such a video follow up connects the name with the face and makes a real impression.

For a more traditional response, remember the famous words of actor Clint Eastwood who warned, "A man's got to know his limitations." So, factoring in the limits of your own time, sort that stack of cards according to value. Choose those three to five treasured connections who can truly be of aid to you and write them something personal, promptly. Add a sentence about what you discussed to help spark that person's memory, until you phone them later. These should be individuals whom you really want to connect with further, for a definite reason. (While you are accepting the card from one of these select luminaries at the meeting, you might demonstrably scribble a note to yourself on it, showing that you don't want to forget her.)

Sort the other cards into "worth a single note." Give these a "nice to have met you" e-mail, using a standard format letter. The remainder, place into a "database only" pile. These get filed through your automatic card reader and sorted out for e-blasts and such.

ATTITUDE ADJUSTMENT. Before you hand it over, think for a moment about what you are giving with your card. Realize that the business card is a small rectangle of hope that you will connect for something beneficial in the future. Determining the realistic odds of that hope will help you determine how far you want to pursue the relationship.

BLUNDERS TO AVOID. Making your own card odd sized gets it more likely tossed than noticed. A picture of your face works only if you are honestly attractive. There are no prizes for the most

words on a card. Clever, cute, attractive are not a business card's aim
– effectively memorable is.

 TIPS & TASKS. Next conference, sort through that stack of cards and take note of those that most catch your interest. Find a few common elements. Then review your own card. **BB**

Beyond Business Branding

Michael Bloomberg – Founder, Bloomberg News Services
Agota S. – Research Chemist, Hoffmann La Roche

When asked how he was able to place his real-time news service so universally around the nation and the globe, Michael Bloomberg responded, "What really sold it was always having more than business on my business site. Every individual – even the most workaholic entrepreneur – has a wealth of outside interests."

We ardently agree, and advocate bringing your whole life's abilities and interests to bear in your business career. No sense using half the shovel.

Examine those varied interests that lasso your passion outside of work. These "outside" interests are worth developing simply to add joy and greater flavor to your life. Cable is stronger and more flexible than a single iron bar because it interweaves many strands. Of course, such interests may directly enhance workplace performance in several ways – greater mental agility, new perspectives, more tenacity, less fear, etc. The human mind, after all, requires more than one kind of work.

Additionally, your passionate diversions may also provide a great avenue of connection that you otherwise might not be able to tap. Letting yourself be known as the office expert on skiing, gardening, or theater history, might seem a bit quirky, at first, but it distinctively brands you as an individual. If nothing else, you rise from "some guy in accounting" to "that guy in accounting who knows everything about the Civil War."

☀ **Branding Yourself.** A good climbing buddy of mine, Agota S., labored with literally hundreds of fellow chemists in the labs of Hoffmann La Roche. On her work station walls were a few pictures of her perched gleefully atop the summits of Mount Rainier and Mount Kilimanjaro, along with several shots of her plastered against a sheer rock face with a climbing rope dangling off into nowhere.

Agota didn't talk about her leisure hours much, but those photos quickly noised her unusual expertise all around the office. Soon coworkers began asking what peak she was going to conquer this weekend. She found herself talking with many higher level research scientists and was even invited to several executive gatherings. And so today, has Agota scaled the corporate heights to take the reins of Hoffmann La Roche? Of course not. But she does state positively that being personally branded often helped the right people give her the proper credit for projects she undertook.

☀ **Work to Play.** Likewise, the reverse branding may bring unexpected windfalls. When gathering up your gear for a bike rally or sampling a new vintage at the Dionysian Society, don't be hesitant to bring in a few interesting anecdotes about your work. Share your full life. You may find beneficial connections flowing in from fellow cyclists and oenophiles. It doesn't hurt to be known as the fellow fishing enthusiast who can prepare my taxes, answer my legal questions, or advise my lazy brother-in-law on finally finding work.

ATTITUDE ADJUSTMENT. Though difficult amid the daily routine, try to perceive yourself and coworkers less as functionaries laboring on a task and more as complete individuals. By learning a person's whole history, or at least some other non-work dimension, you share a perspective. There's a lot less head-butting when people are united by more than just project and job performance.

BLUNDERS TO AVOID. Be modest. Don't brag about your after-hours achievements. If they want to really know the size of the fish or length of the hike, they will ask you. In spinning the latest tale about your diversion, please avoid all exclusive jargon, price, and name dropping. If the story involves a competition, simply remark how exhaustive it all was, not how large was your trophy. Tell less and you'll be asked more.

TIPS & TASKS. Post a few action photos of yourself amidst your favorite diversion. It doesn't hurt to find out who in the executive suites might take interest in your activity.

Most important, become a generous resource. Don't just tell folks you ski, keep ready a list of what slopes are expecting fresh powder this weekend. Like Agota, have a list of clubs with contact information where those interested may get started. You'll be surprised at who comes to your door.

Finally, keep a list of those outside interests of your coworkers and supervisors. Ask for their war stories. **BB**

Telephone Branding

Charlie Walbridge – Owner, Wildwater Designs

"Hello Bart? It's Charlie Walbridge." I can still hear those signature tones rolling across the phone lines like a kindly, gentle thunder. Charlie is a great, muscular barrel of a man, standing somewhere between six-foot-five and 10 feet tall. His undulating basso profundo introduction instantly conjures fond images of hollered greetings on the river, grasping a paddle, and following Charlie's canoe off into spumes of whitewater.

And that is just what he wants you to recall. Owner of Wildwater Designs, Charlie has supplied whitewater rafting and boating enthusiasts with just about every tool and gadget imaginable for fun and survival on America's rivers. Since Wildwater Designs was originally a catalog business, much of the orders and supplier negotiations were done over the phone.

Charlie admits to practicing long and hard to develop just the right phone voice and sculpting certain distinguishing phrases. He sank into selected syllables, slightly elongating them for a rhythmic effect. And it worked. For every moment of the phone conversation, and long after, listeners remember Walbridge's words and the feel of his person. He is verbally branded in their minds.

ATTITUDE ADJUSTMENT. Give folks your verbal essence. How do you want to come across? You may want to harken up images of someone who is friendly, easy to engage, or authoritative, quietly powerful. But above all you want to come across as distinctively yourself. Rather than picking an adjective and trying to match a vocal tone to it, aim for a sound that reminds everyone of just purely you.

BLUNDERS TO AVOID. Never sound busy or hurried. Being busy only impresses listeners with your discourteous disconcern for them. Also, while your initial "Hello" voice can remain the same over years, don't let your distinctive hallmark "you phrases" grow stale. "That's about as useless as tits on a boar," works well for a brief term, but after a few months, find another analogy.

Finally, beware sounding artificial. If you're not a hearty welcoming soul, for heaven's sake don't try to sound like one. You may rehearse, but don't script.

TIPS & TASKS. After developing your phone opening, phrases, and overall tone, record them and listen. Then try out such openings on your spouse or a couple of close, non-business friends. What do they hear? **BB**

Becoming an Expert Witness

Dawn Klotzbeacher – MetLife Executive
Wanda Sano – John Deere & Company Executive

According to U.S. law, an expert witness is a specialist whose knowledge on a subject substantially exceeds that of the average person. The court values such opinions based on their experience and expertise, not necessarily their formal degrees. 'Tis a position to be devoutly sought in one's own firm.

John Deere & Company – 52,000 employees. MetLife – 30,000 employees. Two immense corporate bushels, seemingly vast enough to hide any employee's light, however brilliant. No matter how ambitious one's Horatio Alger urge, struggling up from the clerical level to any sort of prominence in these firms seems about as hopeful as hitting the lottery.

Yet two young women, one in each firm, achieved such a scramble by niching themselves in the same invaluable slot. Each was pretty and poised (definite assets), but neither they nor their parents had the benefit of a college education. Each was very industrious and clever – enough to make the most of an opportunity, but neither was cravenly success-obsessed.

By the mid 1980s all businesses, including Deere and MetLife, were undergoing a process revolution. Everyone saw computers as the necessary wave of the future, but no one was sure exactly what this future would look like, or just what to do with these new gray boxes plunked on their desks.

Opting for the theory of baby steps, both companies began blending computerization into the clerical routine. At this point, both Dawn Klotzbeacher working at MetLife's Elizabeth, New Jersey office, and Wanda Sano, employed at John Deere's Denver office grabbed the reins. While their fellow clerks bemoaned the frustrating labors of adapting to these new whimsical screens, Dawn and Wanda studied. They stayed late and trained.

Soon, each had niched herself as the expert witness in computers. First their fellow employees, then immediate supervisors, and in short order, higher and higher levels of executives sought their aid. Wanda was called to travel and lecture at John Deere offices around the nation and was later promoted into corporate headquarters. Dawn, her capabilities noticed, swiftly rose to a high executive position.

✳ **Project Picking.** "When you're the new kid on the team, you get all the crud jobs," runs the familiar complaint. And, it's often true, since the choice plums are quickly claimed by the seniors, leaving the newbies to rummage through their leavings. But what the seniors pass by often holds equal, if less obvious rewards. This certainly proved true for one young trade magazine editor who was heaped with the assignment covering some new government regulation unenticingly labeled the Occupational Safety and Health Act. Obviously some will o' the wisp, pork-barrel law that everyone would soon quickly ignore, right? Well, the law was not ignored. It not only provided bales of fodder for our young editor's articles, it made him the company expert on this new business factor.

Often these niche projects meet resistance. Agricultural inspector Don Klotzbeacher bucked all department tradition and kept quietly developing new manifest inspection software because it just made sense to him and he saw it as the future. Despite departmental discouagement, he kept at it, until the Secretary of Agriculture called him into his office to acknowledge Don's contribution. (Additionally, his wife, the former Dawn Simpson, provided a great deal of connubial support.)

ATTITUDE ADJUSTMENT. Be prepared to put in considerable extra study and effort on a project that few others initially think worthwhile. The easiest way to handle this, of course, is to choose the right project and believe in it wholeheartedly.

BLUNDERS TO AVOID. Don't silo your information. Keeping your expertise as a personal secret does not make you more essential. It only makes you more annoying. Both Dawn and Wanda freely offered advice and performed quick fix-its for anyone who asked. The more you share, the more your fame as a resource spreads. And people, by and large, repay kindnesses.

Also, don't laurel sit. Whatever field of knowledge you claim as yours, count on new techniques and methods being developed rapidly. Keep up, and keep ahead.

TIPS & TASKS. Make a list of five new projects recently assigned to your department or team. Likewise, examine your workplace's method of operation and come up with three new techniques you have heard about or even invented yourself. Which ones hold that special value that will ride out the test of time? **BB**

Casting a Wider Net

Heinrich Schliemann – Archeologist; Dry Goods Store Owner
Carol Ezzo – Administrative Officer, Prometheus Publishing

Social media stands as virtually living proof that brevity is not necessarily the soul of wit. In fact, it is rather astounding how frequently soporific boredom is achieved in a mere 140 characters – spaces included. This does not mean that your personal interest in any blog or social media (SM) application should be the yardstick for entering it.

Whether you are smitten with the site or find it rather banal is not the point. As a business person you have come to sell your prime asset – yourself – or perhaps to sell your company's product. The real questions about posting SM commercials (that's what they are, after all) must be:

- Does this site take my message to the greatest number of the right people?
- Is my message going to connect with these people?
- Will this connection translate into profits?

☀ **Tempered Expectations.** Having so swiftly and pervasively blasted their way into our culture, blogs and SM remain terribly difficult to assess. We're still reeling a bit from the explosion. No one denies that SM casts your ideas and message to the widest possible numbers of possibly interested individuals. This said, pundits insist that SM alone will not sell your product. Putting aside those wildly touted few who strike instant pay dirt, the actual profits yielded by a broad based SM presence seem to come to those who blend it in as accompaniment to a full, diversified marketing strategy.

Regardless of actual measurement, it cannot be denied that if thousands of folks are daily tweeting about it, certainly brand knowledge and sales are bound to follow. Of course, certain types of products suit this medium better than others. Entertainment, art, food, high consumer goods (e.g., things found in a mall), and small purchases tend to garner more SM-related sales than homes, generators, or yachts. On the other hand, if your fun U-Tube links can set folks drooling over your yachts, it may work wonders. Then check competitors and examine their results.

The really good news: You are the ideal product for SM show casing. Blog and SM visitors generally are looking more for intriguing individuals than for stuff. So feel free to center the content of your own blog and site around yourself and your firm's people.

✳ **Commandments of Content.** Four hints on what to write and how:

1. In all postings, be brief, consistent, and dependably frequent. Create informational/story threads that inspire people to follow and to constantly check back with your SM site or blog. This differs markedly from the canned messages now so popular with SM services. These latter are merely repetitive rephrasings of the same old, same old. Yeech. The former informational/story threads build what every author strives for: a page-turning sense of suspense.

2. Provide value to the reader. Social media is a gold rush – not a gold mine. Your best bet is to put down your pick and concentrate on providing your millions of fellow miners with the tools they need. Readers should be saying, "Hey, that sounds interesting," or "That's news I can use and profit from." Before posting, look at each offering from a reader's POV and ask, "What's in this for me?"

Humble grocer's clerk Heinrich Schliemann landed on the shores of California in 1849 originally intent on seeking gold. Instead, after seeing the real demand, he sold all his equipment, ordered more, and set up an equipment store that supplied everyone else in the camp. Mr. Schliemann made millions overnight. He later used this wealth to lead archeological expeditions that unearthed Homer's fabled city of ancient Troy. What can your SM words give that will build a following of folks wanting to buy from you?

3. Avoid direct selling. Social Mediaites generally cherish the delusion that they are individually discovering things, rather than being sold to from an external force. They do not want to feel that they are being hit by a commercial, even if they are. Thus terms like "check out this…", or "tasted & liked this… ," which lead them to a video or some other site will lower the audience's innate, and justified sales resistance.

4. Be entertaining. Nothing beats humor. (That's what initially sold the internet to millions of first time users.) Clever wordings, quippy quotes all work. Social media writing is mostly a batch of headlines – take the time and make them catchy.

ATTITUDE ADJUSTMENT. Be patient. The pace may be fast, but results build only with time. Computer guru and serial blog founder Carol Ezzo notes that people have so many sites available to them, and so many postings on each site, that regardless of content, it will take a while for you to get noticed. "Take heart," she says, "it only takes a few people to spread the word, yet it also takes time."

BLUNDERS TO AVOID. SM demands more time and less money than any type of marketing imaginable. So forget the myth about it being "free marketing." Be prepared to spend unpredictable oceans of your most precious resource – your time. Of course, for the entrepreneur for whom it is her sole resource, SM is ideal.

You may, to a certain extent, relegate your SM duties to a professional. Just make sure that this pro is not charging you $1000 a month to send messages that your existent sales staff can easily craft and clerk-level administrator can post.

TIPS & TASKS. Simplify Simplify. SM abounds with nearly limitless sites, each with an amazing array of newsfeeds and daunting aspects that can set you on endlessly complex chases. Instead, query colleagues and competitors. There are no cookie-cutter answers to social media. Test the waters with a few applications to which you can conveniently contribute. Monitor them. Keep a list of each site, its number of views, and resulting website visits, if possible. Then experiment further. And above all, have some fun with this. SM is designed to bring people to people. So explore and search out some new folks with whom to chat. Enjoy. **BB**

Building Word Style

A strong verbal agility, oracular mobility, conversant facility, vocabularistic capability shall magnify your true abilities and exacerbate your esteem.

Or you could say: increased word power allows you to sell yourself and to think better.

Each expresses roughly the same concept. And there is a time for each. The former, Gilbert-and-Sullivan style phrasing is more poetic and fun than the boring, lowbrow explanation. And although not readily memorizable, it certainly is memorable to the ear. What a marvelous style to break the boredom of an annual accounting report. The second version hits harder and makes the statement's truth settle in more poignantly. But whatever your form of expression, you have to have the right words at your tongue tip to make a commanding presence.

✳ **Wordsmithing.** This goes way far beyond the discipline of learning three new words each week. It is the continuing quest to express yourself in a more interesting and precise way. As a self-marketer, you should ever be creating new taglines that describe what you do. Statistician Alan Wilson keeps an unending supply ranging from "I supply facts to support people's preconceived prejudices," to "I give people data so they can manipulate it toward their desired conclusions."

Sometimes generality creates intrigue, such as the author who announces that "I write stuff." Other times simplified exactness hits the mark, "the wheels on the Mars robot require motion sensors, and they pay me to put them there."

✳ **Mind Razoring.** We think in words. Each of us employs words, whether we are communicating our business visions and concepts to ourselves, or to others. A greater vocabulary simply arms you with more and sharper tools for forging that vision into reality.

Don't silo your information. Keeping your expertise secret does not make you more essential. It only makes you more annoying.

If you can determine the difference between an argument's gist, its essence, and its bottom line, you will hold a great advantage in judging its value.

ATTITUDE ADJUSTMENT. After you consider what you want to say, pause and think of the most effective wording for it. When asked about his latest summit one climber concisely summed it up as "physically rugged and spiritually rich." The words are poetic and lyrically matched and they provide an image stronger than an ocean of adjectives.

BLUNDERS TO AVOID. There is no prize for the use of large or confusing words. Enlarge your vocabulary as a method of communicating, not impressing folks with your erudition.

TIPS & TASKS. Browse through magazines and books whose style attracts and rivets your attention. Rather than plagiarizing their phrases for your own, study their style, pick out the elements that make it effective. **BB**

Afterthoughts

❋ Try the Three/Ten Rule. Limit yourself to mentioning three personal achievements in every 10 minutes of conversation. Nothing is more off-putting than the patter of little feats.

❋ Lure the quarry to you. In each encounter, actively seek out the deeds and masteries of others first. Let them ask about you in good time.

❋ How many more people have learned of your abilities this week? Branding yourself is an ongoing discipline. No product succeeds when sold to just one customer.

❋ Nothing so impresses people as quiet, understated confidence. That is because it cannot be assumed or feigned. It is an aura which must radiate from within.

❋ Don't strive to be "above" selling your excellence. You will only garner resentment as others less able and more aggressive climb past you.

❋ Do you like the way you look and sound when telling others about yourself? Hmm. What do you suppose could be done about that?

❋ Boss, client, coworkers – there are a few specific individuals whom you must impress with your abilities. But after that, it is a numbers game. Reach out and subtly cast bread on all the waters.

❋ Others praising your achievements is always best. But this only blossoms if you plant the seed.

BB

CHAPTER 6

Final Caveats

*No matter what you ask for, you will be envisioning a mansion,
while your builder is hammering out a bungalow.*

Prelude

Normally, this would be the end. While the quest for individual improvement within the business realm goes ever onward, we had planned to wrap up our symphony of business tactics on an upbeat note. (Then finish with the successful self-selling tips of the previous chapter.)

Several visually oriented folks voted for more cartoons. Yet the one constant theme that came through was a gentle disgruntlement that we had painted the world of business too rosily. Looking back, we stand guilty as charged – with an explanation. First, we honestly believe that business is exhilarating. It affords unrivaled avenues for human creativity. More importantly, by shifting into a positive attitude, you create a better pathway for achievement. No one grinds her way joylessly to success.

Yet admittedly, all roads in business lie studded with enormous obstacles and frequent enemies plotting your downfall. This chapter holds to light some of these hurdles. It also provides some methods for reshaping yourself to deal with them more effectively. As always, the pivotal factor is You. Many of these problems stand ongoing and immutable. You cannot escape or bulldoze them away. Yet, by refusing to revel in your rage and concentrating on ways to get what you need, you may just find a way to better finesse or endure the challenges.

Everybody Overcharges & Under Delivers

Back in 1841, author Edgar Allen Poe wrote a hilarious, all-too-true account of his trying to pry payment from a belligerently obstinate publisher. Poe failed. Such has always been the way of the business world.

✧ Today, we have officialized this insolent delay with popular accounting software programmed to schedule payment on the last day before lawsuits kick in.

✧ Annually, thousands of startups fail, not for want of business, but because their clients string out payment until the new, cash-starved company collapses and dies broke.

✧ Ask a fellow team member to collaborate on your report and odds are you'll be knocking on his door Wednesday trying to get the papers that were due Tuesday.

✧ Tell your web developer that your new website doesn't flow seamlessly and he will condescendingly smile and, with manifest in hand, tell you that he has built every element for which you have asked.

✧ And when was the last time you heard a contractor say "I gave you a little extra over here because I thought you could use it"?

And so it goes. You can virtually count on the quality being not up to your standards, delivered behind time, and the whole thing sticky-noted with add-on charges. At the same time you cannot run a career or business with things substandard. So what's a business person to do?

✳ **Great Expectations.** No one is going to build to your fantasy, and probably not even construct it up to your standards. No matter what you actually ask for, you will be envisioning a mansion, while the builder is hammering out a bungalow. Your only hope is to strive for an exact mutual understanding.

Such a connection between buyer and builder necessarily goes beyond any written contract. It begins, ideally, with a face-to-face discussion of the project, entailing intense listening and reading of body language. If Jim seems hesitant about getting his share of the report to you on time, or Melissa shies away from actually being able to construct this piece of the website in exactly that way, note it down. Don't challenge them on it yet, wait until the end of your discussion.

Prior to this buyer/builder exchange, create a list of "must haves" for the project. What items must meet the utmost standards of precision? Where can you cut a little slack? Then, as you are talking, adjust your list as needed. Finally, as you wrap up this discussion, present him with the Must Have list. Make things infinitely clear. Also, now is the time to politely question him about those hesitancies you noted earlier and gauge his response. Allow your fantasies to slide into a more realistic picture, which hopefully this builder can meet. If he cannot perform as needed, it may be time to look elsewhere.

✳ **Other People's Ethics.** For many individuals, holding back on cash due and providing as little as they can get away with seems simply good business. Carried to the extreme, such practices range from ethically dubious to downright underhanded, but there are definite fiscal advantages. The later I give you my money, the longer I have it to use myself. The less service and accessories I give you in a product, the less I must spend to get your business.

And this strictly-cash-flow approach to business works – provided you can endure a Thrift-only reputation. In the end, success hinges on the reputation of both the product and the company dispensing it. When you make it very clear that cash is your sole aim, you will soon find equally cynical buyers interested only in price.

If, like Walmart, Home Depot, and the scores of burger chains nationwide, you can meet these lowest-price expectations, you'll get a hefty chunk of the market and no one will ask questions. But remember your niche. If you plan to offer levels of service or cannot beat the low-price boys, you are aiming for a different market share and your customers will hold you to a higher standard. They will not accept hidden cost overruns, late or sloppy service.

✷ **The Baker's Dozen.** In the face of ethically shady, cut-rate, and downright illegal scams used by competitors to pirate your business, temptations are great. But if that style doesn't fit your nature, you'll probably succeed better by turning their failings to your advantage. Three decades ago, when the retail clothing landscape consisted mainly of cavernous, impersonal superstores, small clothing boutiques sprang up and made a killing. They offered more, and so can you.

Counter the Thrift-only reputation with one of service and personal generosity. Like the neighborhood bakers of old who used to put in thirteen pastries and call it a dozen, an investment in a little extra pays back exponentially in return customers. Yet such generosity works only if it is matched by an equally generous persona. That additional service, item, or bit of labor must be seen as coming from someone with a truly giving nature.

ATTITUDE ADJUSTMENT. Temper your visions as a buyer with reality. What can actually be built, on budget, in reasonable time? An increase in your need does not increase the possibility of getting it done better or sooner.

Stand foursquare against the competitive practices you deplore. Present yourself visibly as the kind of individual you want to seen as – and act that way. This may mean paying bills promptly when cash is tight, being scrupulously honest in fulfillment, and smiling when that extra service feels like you're giving away the store.

BLUNDERS TO AVOID. Do not denigrate competitors or coworkers who follow a different path than yours. Nothing turns off others as thoroughly as hearing from you how everybody else has taken the low road, while your company stands ever on the moral high ground.

TIPS & TASKS. Pull the mote out of your own eye. Examine your own practices for quality and promptness of fulfillment, cash payment, and services offered. Are you in an "everybody does it mode" of which you may or may not approve? **BB**

Devil in Details

Donald Trump – Chairman, CEO, The Trump Organization
Steve Miller – Founder, Miller Damon Construction

Donald Trump used to laughingly wave around what he called his "$100,000 piece of paper." It was a little niggling rider that he would sneak into his real estate deals that caught most buyers completely off guard. Right before negotiating a deal, Trump would type up a brief paragraph and insert it into the contract, stating, in essence, that the property to be sold was, and would continue to be, handled by the Trump Management Company, owned by guess who?

This contract, among other duties, offered The Donald a percentage of all the rents he collected before turning them over to the new owner. If buyers wanted to opt out of this tie with Trump Management, they need only pay a severance fee of $100,000. Most buyers, less than enthralled with the thought of Mr. Trump fingering their rents, gladly ponied up the extra fee.

All of us know similar stories. Phone companies used to offer credit cards which, somewhere in the contract, included a switch of service provider. One major document-sharing service buries within its 35-page agreement the right for the service to publish any of the shared documents anywhere it wishes, with no royalties.

Steve Miller, founder of Miller Damon Construction in Manhattan summed it up beautifully. "I wouldn't sign my own contract, but I'm pleased as punch when anybody else does." Call it sharp business practice or white collar theft, such deliberately buried cash-extraction clauses are an aged aspect of commerce.

Instead of debating the ethics, make yourself wary. Unfortunately, being forewarned does not make you forearmed. So many written and spoken agreements swirl around most of us daily that we cannot ferret out every snare. But here are a few tips:

1. **The bigger the company, the more likely its agreements hold clever cash-extraction clauses.** This is not because large corporations are inherently corrupt. They are not. They simply have more people working on each deal. They can afford to have experienced pros who word each contract to the company's utmost advantage. The small firm is so happy to get the business that it is likely to download a boilerplate agreement and send it on for signature.

2. **Find comparatives.** If you are frequently buying a lot of one kind of supply or offering a set service to a specific class of buyer, it's worth checking the industry for standard, acceptable agreements. Note language and popular phrasings. Particularly, notice the length of paragraphs that cover certain topics. If some new agreement section takes thrice the words as is typical, give it a careful reading.

3. **Seek professional and nonprofessional help.** The easiest way to check over any proposed agreement is to contact referrals who've dealt with the company. When asking about the quality of work, promptness, etc., be sure to check if they encountered furtive details that separated them from a few extra bucks. Of course, if you have an attorney and accountant on retainer, by all means employ their expertise. If the fees seem a bit high for mere contract review, try your area's Small Business Development Center which can link you with free mentors and low cost legal aid.

ATTITUDE ADJUSTMENT. Become a detail-oriented person. Regardless of your job or the type of your business, no successful person can delegate details. If you can read, you can handle most contracts. It just takes careful scrutiny. So establish a quiet time and place, and set your concentration to the task. You will find it is a discipline that spreads benefit throughout your career.

BLUNDERS TO AVOID. Don't shatter good will with paranoia. In all your dealings, be they with associates old or new, assume their total honesty and act accordingly. Yes, be wise and study the agreement or contract back in your office, but when discussing the venture with them, always indicate that they have your complete trust.

If you discover some version of the Trump $100,000 clause hiding in the contract, don't tackle its author around the knees and bring him thudding to earth. Simply note that "I was having some trouble with page 3, could you explain it to me?"

TIPS & TASKS. Business is won as well as lost in the details. Review other contracts and terms and agreement sheets. Are there clever aspects that you should be including in your business negotiations? **BB**

Impossible S.O.B.s

Michael Griffith – CEO, Laureate Biopharmaceutical Services, Inc.
Chris Illuminati – Author, **A**hology – The Art of Getting**
What You Want and Getting Away With It

All business is personal and some persons are a lot more annoying than others. In work, as in life, you can count on encountering those individuals whom you simply loathe and who, deliberately or inadvertently, make your day a living hell.

"Helen" had a gift for spreading unhappiness wherever she went. She sat on the board of directors, reveling in her unofficial power base as wife of the board's strongest member. Helen actually disliked the company, its workers, and its product. She was famous for such quotes as, "I don't think any of the employees should get a raise. They should consider themselves lucky to have a job."

And as for customers, she queried, "We need the absolute minimum counter staff. How long can we keep a customer waiting before he will leave without buying?" She even invited herself to the employee staff meetings where she ever attempted to take charge. Helen's hubby supported her unenlightened micromanagement, to the resentment of all.

❋ **Judo Management.** The company CEO, "Lorraine" was at her wit's end. Like so many of us, she was snared under the authority of a person in power who stymied her every attempt to take the company forward. But after a few weeks of nightly tooth grinding, Lorraine developed a non-homicidal plan. Helen's hubby always had his eye on prestige enhancement. It was his primary drive.

So Lorraine decided to use the thrust of that force and redirect it slightly for the good of the company. She kept repeating to all board members at their meetings what great supporters of the business they were, how they were contributing to the firm, the industry, and society at large. They should be proud of themselves each time the company took a step forward.

Slowly, painfully, the board, including Helen and her hubby, began to believe that the company and its prosperity was the key to what they valued most – their own prestige. They began making speeches in public about how they were working for the firm and a more enlightened society. Everyone applauded. So they made more speeches. Then Lorraine sprung the trap. She made proposals based on their promises. And, whether by belief or for the sake of image maintenance, they backed them.

✳ **Team Misfits.** "I don't tolerate them," says Michael Griffith. "The moment I spot an individual who is not working with the team, for the company's total benefit, he is gone. I don't care if he is the top scientist or top producer. Success comes from groups."

Mr. Griffith's theories of success have borne fruit. In 1997, he founded the Chirex, Inc. pharmaceutical firm from nothing and in four years sold it for a cool $520 million. His second venture, Aptuit, Inc. proved equally, rapidly profitable.

When you come to work for one of Michael Griffith's companies, you do not come to make a name for yourself or politic your way upward. You come to work. And if you cannot work and play well with others, you will be swiftly invited, in Griffith's terms, to "go find a group somewhere else in which you may find happiness."

No career coddler, Griffith's race to success allows for only amputation, not prolonged and gentle healing. Executives who spot a canker in the team, however, do have a choice. They may, and should, size up this individual and determine the problem. It might just be, in fact, that they are the sole individual working for the company's benefit and the rest of the team is askew. Is there a possible healing for this person? Or is it time to invite him or her to seek happiness elsewhere?

ATTITUDE ADJUSTMENT. Ask yourself, "Why do I loathe this individual?" Then answer honestly. Frequently, resentment plays a vital role in such hatreds. It's not that John does things wrong or greedily, but that he has been given the position and power to act that way and screw things up. Author Chris Illuminati divides our human culture into the 90 percent "nice guys" and 10 percent much-envied "A**holes." The latter is the guy who walks briskly into the club while you obediently wait behind the velvet cord; who has no trouble getting the bartender or boss's attention while you quietly wait to be noticed.

Setting aside Mr. Illuminati's labels for a moment, there is some wisdom in developing a stance where you base your actions on what you want, rather than on your perception of others' opinion. Go ahead, break a few eggs. Live for yourself and let greedy John stumble on his own path.

BLUNDERS TO AVOID. Do not carry tales or share gossip about annoying people. This is a hard one. But you don't win by sharing your ill feelings. Rumor is a serpent who makes the bearer as despised as the tale he carries.

TIPS & TASKS. Review your work history and list the people with whom you have not gotten along. Look for their common traits, then ask what this reveals about you. What do you need to adjust to work better? One woman who did this drill discovered, to her total surprise, that she held an immense bias towards overweight people. **BB**

Hard Times

Henry Steinway – Founder, Steinway & Sons Pianos
Paul Dorf – Managing Director, Compensation Resources, Inc.

This book is being written and read during our nation's worst recession since the 1930s. Overall, the picture is bleak and everyone is both feeling the pinch and loudly letting out his individual yelp. You will find no stoicism in this recession.

Times are almost, though not quite as bad, as they were at the outset of the American Civil War. By 1862, the federal government appeared in a teetering shambles. In the first Battle of Bull Run, a totally defeated Union Army had chaotically retreated to Washington in disorder. Many residents expected to see Robert E. Lee's Confederate troops riding up to the White House to demand Mr. Lincoln's surrender. Union General McClellan had denied his Commander in Chief's order to attack. Thousands of businesses had shut down, money was more than tight, food was scarce.

Meanwhile, that very year in New York, burgeoning piano maker Henry Steinway began work on the first Steinway Hall whose over 2,000 seats would, upon completion, make it the Big Apple's largest concert auditorium. Mr. Steinway and his sons had sold 483 pianos to date. "It is our superior product, not the economy, that has made the time proper for this enormous step," he was heard to say.

Down in Philadelphia that year, the hard pressed industrialists and merchants founded the Union League with the motto "Love of Country Leads." They pooled funds and erected the gracious, elegant Union League Hall. Today, it still stands as a grand American monument to the refusal to knuckle under to hard times.

❋ **Long Term Prep.** Perhaps it is due to the media's greater focus on the whiners, but one does not see Americans taking this latest economic downturn very well. Largely, this is because many folks are not viewing the times as hard. Rather, they see today and this quarter as a brief, temporary abnormality that some villains created, and some good people should get on the stick and instantly fix. We want the anti-recession pill.

When President Franklin Delano Roosevelt spoke to the people concerning the 1930s Great Depression, his audience expected long, hard days and drudging years before improvement. Eight decades later when President Barrack Obama spoke before the nation at his inaugural, he repeatedly noted that the way back up would be an agonizing, slow process. Everyone nodded, but very few believed.

So regardless of what you individually think of this or that administration's handling of our economy, there are a few bitter facts whose realization will better direct your actions:

1. Blame is irrelevant to your business or your career. Astutely fixing this recession's fault will not turn red ink to black or get you a job.
2. Hard times settle unevenly and unfairly over the landscape. They tend to squat and stay for long spells and disappear gradually.
3. Guaranteed. After we "get back on track" from this downturn, more hard times will settle in, sometime down the road. A little provident saving and preparation beforehand makes a better plan than counting on some clever tactical shift mid-disaster.

ATTITUDE ADJUSTMENT. Build a Union League Hall instead of a cave. "Too many of us today," says Paul Dorf, founder of Compensation Resources, Inc., have fallen into what I call the lockdown, siege mentality. People become afraid to hire, afraid to make moves. They take on the attitude that any change is bad. In fact, more now than ever, today is not the death knell."

It is wise to be cautious with your funds, but not with your vision. If you can make yourself believe that today, like any other, holds opportunities in your field, you can set yourself hunting them out, just as you would when skies are less gray.

BLUNDERS TO AVOID. Beware of the maxim that radical times call for radical measures. It may be the time to stride forth and build a Steinway Hall, or more likely, it's time to merely learn what would better serve your clients or your supervisor.

TIPS & TASKS. Assess exactly your own situation during these hard times. Forget the traumas of the real estate industry or Pakistan stock market. How hard are you hit individually, in your industry, in your community? Now, set aside the percent of business lost and how good things were before. Consider where things stand today – your income and revenue. Can you survive on that? Then with this base in mind, list steps that would increase that cash flow. Be sure to include the time and expense of each step. **BB**

Guarding Your Soul

Jean-Paul Sartre – Existentialist Philosopher

Onslaughts against the real you come from all over, in increasingly subtle and numerous ways. That magical, internal essence of your own true self is a thing to be nurtured and cherished. Expressing it is the only way you will find any satisfaction in life. However, society sternly instructs us from the moment we take our first breaths that this essence is a thing to be subverted. Everyone has plans for it, and theirs, we're told, are much better and wiser than your own plans for yourself.

One of the main reasons for business burnout is that our inner soul can be denied for only so long. Generations of men and women have been taught to labor on "the company's time" at any task some other person deems necessary. It may be any task – performed for any person properly titled. You have bartered a major piece of your life for cash, and now they want you to love what they would have you do. Even the hope of joy in such situations sounds surreal.

Fortunately, today, the trend is turning toward considering people as a company's prime asset and the provable link between employee happiness and production is recognized. In truth, you alone must be the sole guardian of your inner self and desires. After all, only you know what makes you happy and how to pursue it. But in the midst of your business turmoil, allow us to offer you a few final tips.

* **Avoid Role Play.** We have all seen that waiter, who rather than being Dave who brings your food as Dave would, casts himself in a caricature of that position. He nods, pours, poses, repeats the oh-so-proper phrases. Rather than find fulfillment in his work, Dave has chosen to operate by some perceived set of rules that he wears as gracefully as a pudgy opera diva in a miniskirt.

   It takes some diligent work, but it is worth the self-examination to monitor your own daily work motions and catch yourself impersonating the very model of a modern marketing manager, engineer, tech service person, etc. Great release and satisfaction come from banishing these restrictive roles. Further, it leads toward developing recognized self-branding and a more unfettered pathway to success.

* **Set Aside Sartre Time.** French existentialist philosopher Jean-Paul Sartre was renowned for depicting the delicacy of one's personal essence and the impossibility of maintaining it within a constant social swirl. He often cited the case of how an individual might experience a pond in a wood in truly his own way. Yet the instant one other person was spotted across the pond, the entire experience would change.

   To bring all your own undistracted creativity to bear on both your life and your business, set aside some totally alone time. Make it long enough to breathe away all the cares, thorny phrases, and multitude of "shoulds," and naturally, effortlessly let your soul out of hiding. Once it's free, you may let it roam, or direct it toward specific challenges. Your choice. Your re-creation time.

☀ **Take Reality Checks.** A huge muscular man stands quivering before a harsh, berating, slender-framed man whom the former could crush with a single blow. Yet he does not. Some imagined, mutual social bond has made the large man put on smiles and looks of contrition and feel grateful for this minimal punishment as he bows to take on more assigned labor.

I witnessed this scene in a slave mine in South Africa, yet it could just as well describe a scene in your own workplace. I am not suggesting that every large worker pummel his smaller supervisor. But it does help to stand back periodically and ask yourself why you are racing like a rat in a maze. Is this particular task really necessary? How necessary? What is its place within my life? This perspective may serve to further motivate or reprioritize what you're doing.

ATTITUDE ADJUSTMENT. Take time and seek out that inner essence of you – your soul. Get to know you a little better, apart from your fellows, and the many strictures on your time and thought. If you're not finding a very likable person, look harder. He or she is in there, and it is this person you want to carefully bring out and present to others. They will be pleased at your sincerity and work will flow more easily.

BLUNDERS TO AVOID. Beware that your perceived essence is not really a reaction to others' behavior. "They are all unethical, I am not." Or "I am easy going, they are cutthroat." Determine who you are, not who you aren't.

TIPS & TASKS. Use happiness as a litmus test. Does being in a certain situation or doing a certain thing bring you happiness – as opposed to just relief or pleasure? Then odds are it's part of your make up. Guard it well. ▪▪

Afterthoughts

✳ If only one person can spoil for you an entire team filled with friends and allies, does that reflect worse on him – or you?

✳ There is a certain remedy in ignoring bitter circumstance. Those who deny fate seem much more likely to rise above it.

✳ Times were always better; business always easier to launch; others were always richer and more morally pure. And today everyone else has the competitive edge. Stop comparing; start moving.

✳ Perhaps the only sure advantage is to operate as if you don't deserve anything.

✳ Motivational guarantees do not exist. But you might ask yourself, "How hard would I work for a person who treats people like I do?"

✳ Companies pay money for honest labor and for misreading cleverly written contracts. This is why business demands both hard working hands and heads.

✳ "The surest guarantee of failure is to plan for it. The companies I see succeed are the ones who make every step as if success is a certainty." – *Michael Griffith*

✳ It is easy to control a person when you know what he truly wants. After that, it's merely a matter of dangling the carrot in the right direction.

✳ The way may not always be rosy, but odds are, you'll be a lot more satisfied contributing your brain and back in a business, than lounging on the couch.

ABOUT BartsB**oo**ks

BartsBooks is the outgrowth of my great business information frustration. During 25+ years as a business journalist, I witnessed increasingly less practical, helpful, and concise presentations of this information. This frustration led me to design a process for a series of collaboratively written business guides.

After interviewing thousands of specialists, I figured if one expert could provide a few really good solutions, several scores of experts, all focused on the same challenge could truly give you the tools you need. This is the essence of BartsBooks. Each of our Ultimate Business Guides distills and precisely conveys proven solutions from seasoned professionals that might just answer the prayers of those struggling with some aspect of business.

The focus and direction of each guide is determined by proven business Authorities. Each Book In Progress is then posted on www.BartsBooks.com to allow online contributors opportunities to post pertinent experiences, ideas, and insights.

Once the deadline to post has passed, our editors weave Authorities' wisdom and experience with ideas solicited from online contributors. The result is a series of concise, practical, nugget-laden business guides, available in both hard cover and eBook formats, on www.BartsBooks.com.

Those who contribute their ideas are given a Personal Page to highlight their contact information. In addition, this page contains a complete anthology of their BartsBooks contributions which may be forwarded to clients, colleagues, friends, and social media contacts.

Our Vision

We believe each individual harbors an innate craving to create things for the good; and business offers an unrivaled avenue for unleashing this force. At BartsBooks, we strive to:

☀ Ignite excitement for business

☀ Share mutual expertise

☀ Provide practical tools for commerce
   and industry

☀ Offer opportunities for individuals to showcase
   their proficiencies.

We are thrilled to be able to provide a platform that supports this process.

To learn more, and to contribute your ideas, please visit www.BartsBooks.com

We look forward to your insights,

– Bart Jackson